The Horror of My Thoughts

The Horror of My Thoughts
A Visit to Auschwitz & Birkenau

Photo Illustrations and Text by
Nat Crosby

Winnisimmet Press Chelsea Massachusetts

This book was set in Century Gothic and Trajan Pro
Printed and Bound in the United States of America
by Lulu.com

ISBN-13 978-0-578-00140-1

Winnisimmet Press
165 Winnisimmet St. #2D
Chelsea MA 02150

www.winnisimmetpress.com

TO MY GRANDPARENTS:
HERMEL AND IRENE MARTIN
LUTHAN AND PATRICIA CROSBY
THANK YOU

Forward

I found myself traveling through the Polish countryside on my way to Auschwitz. I was unprepared for this journey, not because I lacked time, but because I refused to prepare myself for visiting a death camp of the Holocaust. I would not listen when others around me talked in anticipation of our visit. Selfishly, I wondered how I would function in the immediate future. How would I react, that afternoon the rest of the day, or week, to a place I did not know? I recognized however, that it was imperative to go.

On arriving, I began to photograph and found that I could not. I tried to sketch, and could not. The horror of my roving eyes and mind were so strong. I began again to photograph, for I felt I must.

Unknowingly, rather than the near future only, I was going to be profoundly affected by this place forever. Affected by not just what happened, but also by how I reacted to Auschwitz within my thoughts.

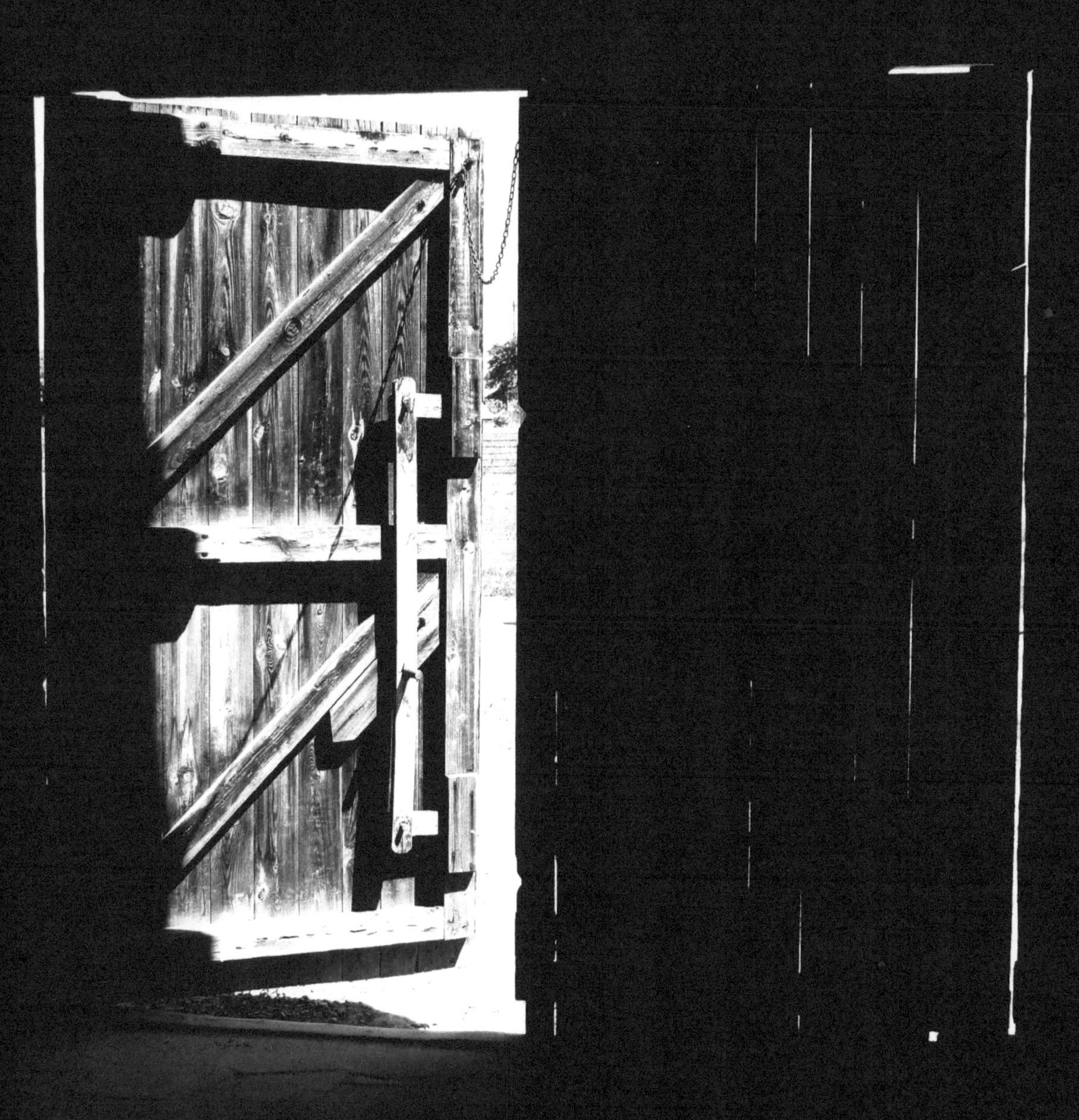

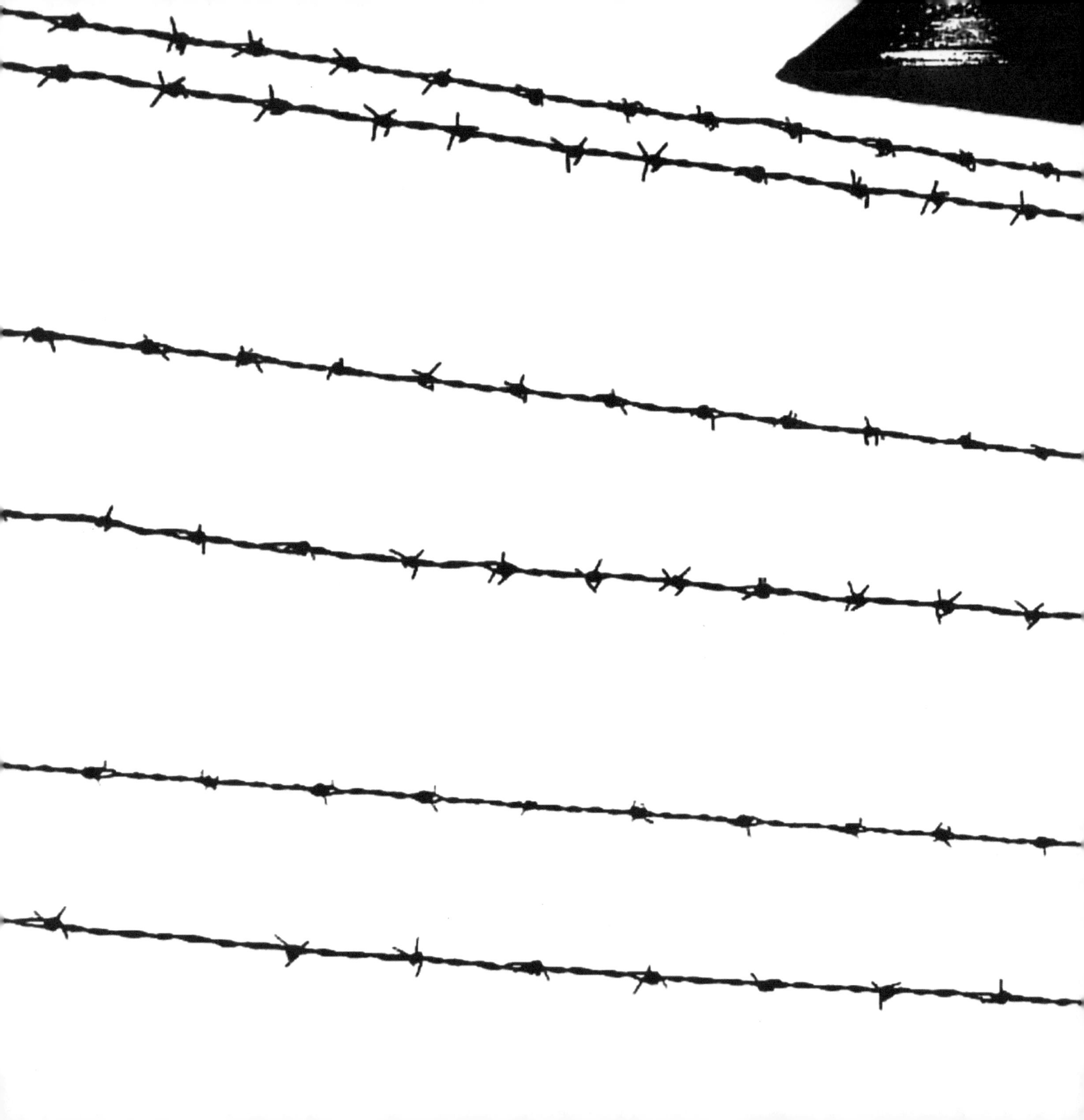

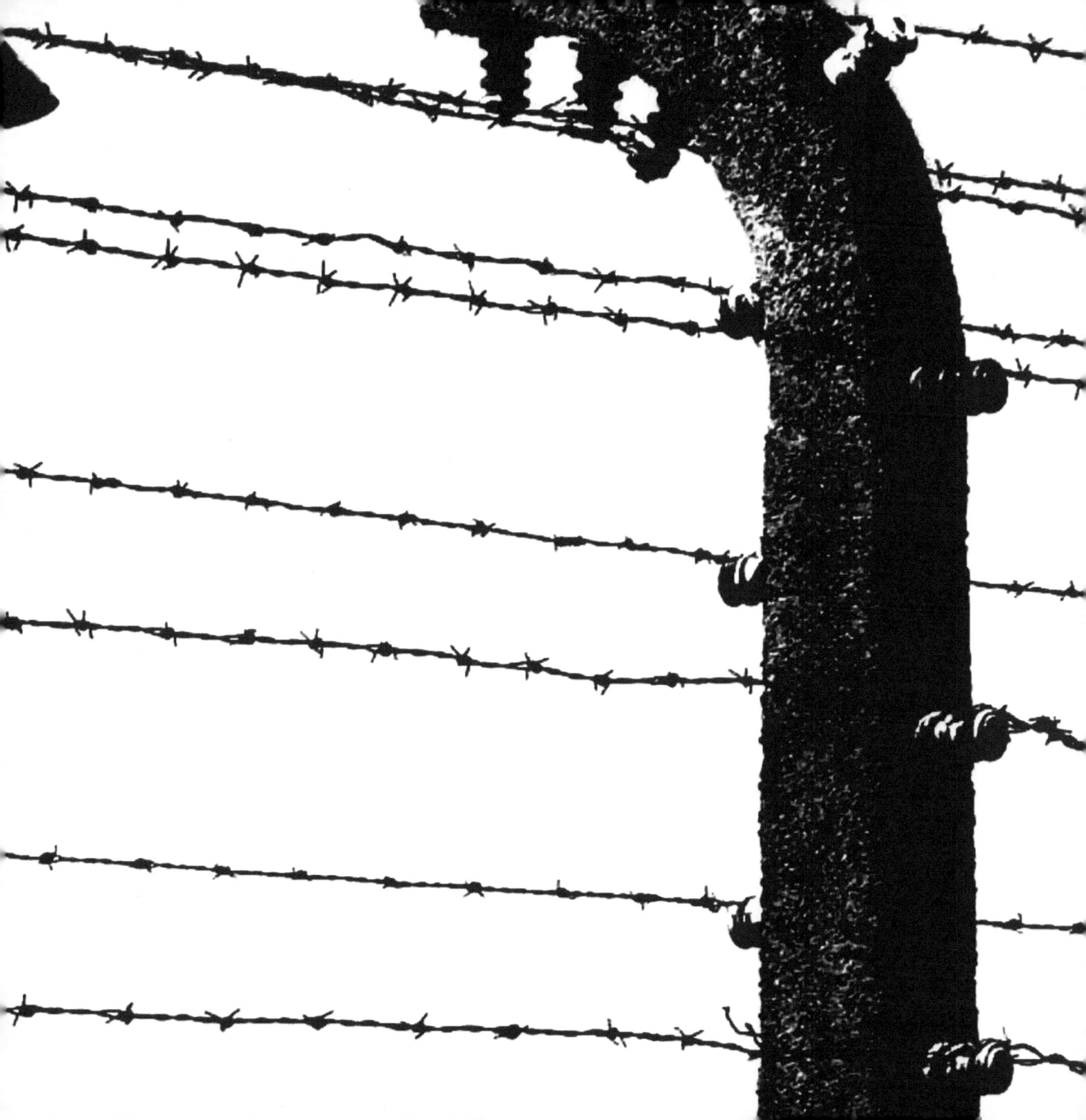

Introduction

First, my thoughts wandered, desperately trying to avoid thinking about where I was. Auschwitz felt ironic in its contradictions, at times beautiful in its physicality, and then infused with horror and disgust in its reality.

Like black and white flashing in my head, the thoughts came between the barrage of the tour guides pale and unceasing voice.

The Horror of My Thoughts
A visit to Auschwitz & Birkenau

As early as 1919 Jews were being blamed for Germany's defeat[1] in WWI. A new political party arose from anti-Semitism, the National Socialist German Workers Party, the NSDAP; called the "Nazi party." One of the early members, Adolf Hitler, spoke on "Why we are against the Jews," promising that his party "will free you from the power of the Jew."[2] At first the Nazi party and Hitler were ignored, —in part due to their marginal popularity— but on Jan. 30, 1933 Hitler was appointed Chancellor[3] to Germany. Disregarding the Locarno Pact, Germany invades the Rheinland in early March 1936, with little international reaction. Three years later, in August, the Nazi-Soviet Nonaggression Pact is signed, followed by the invasion of Poland by Germany. On September 3, Britain and France declared war on Germany. By the end of the month[4] Poland is partitioned between Germany and the Soviet Union. World War II has begun.

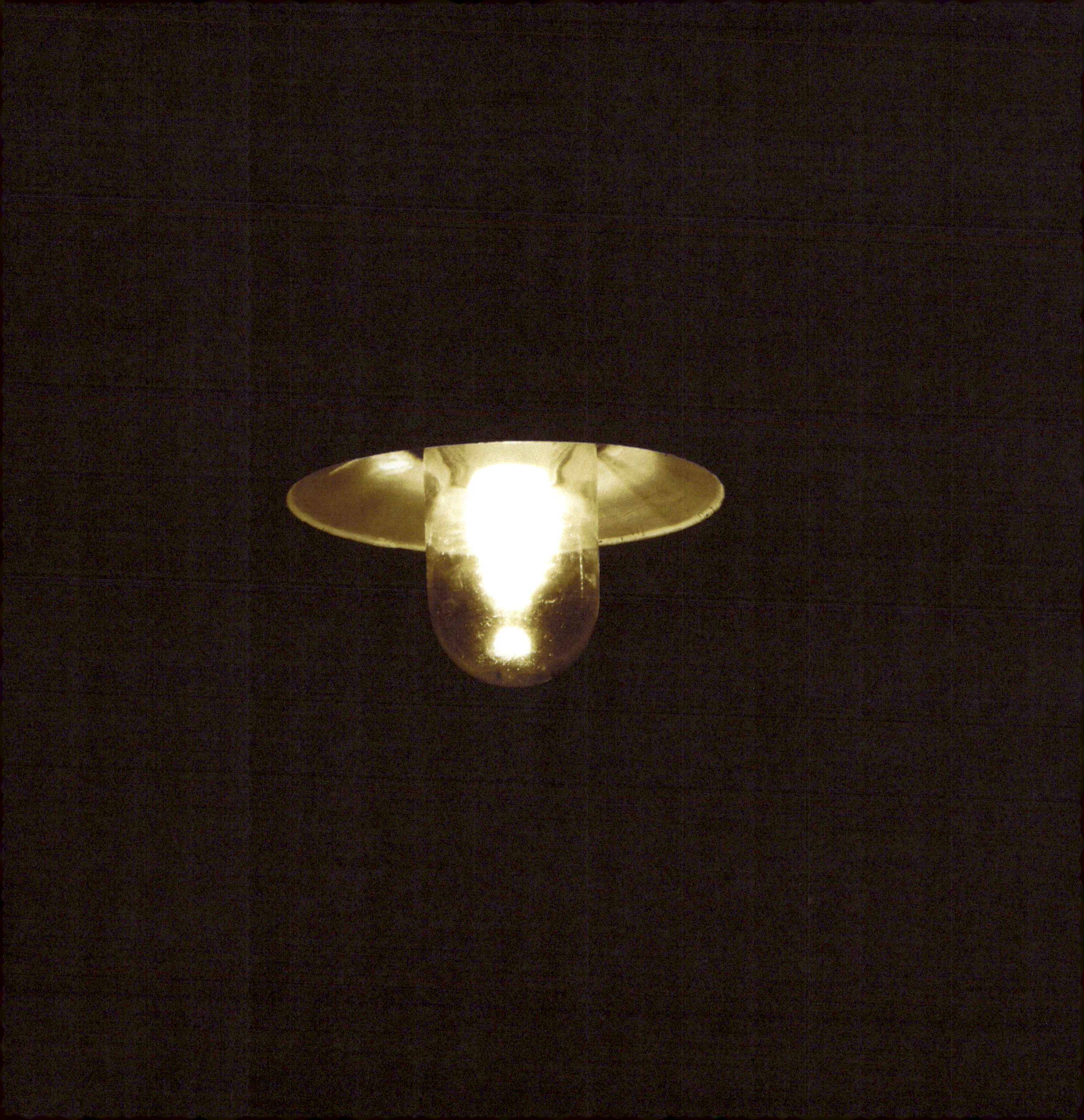

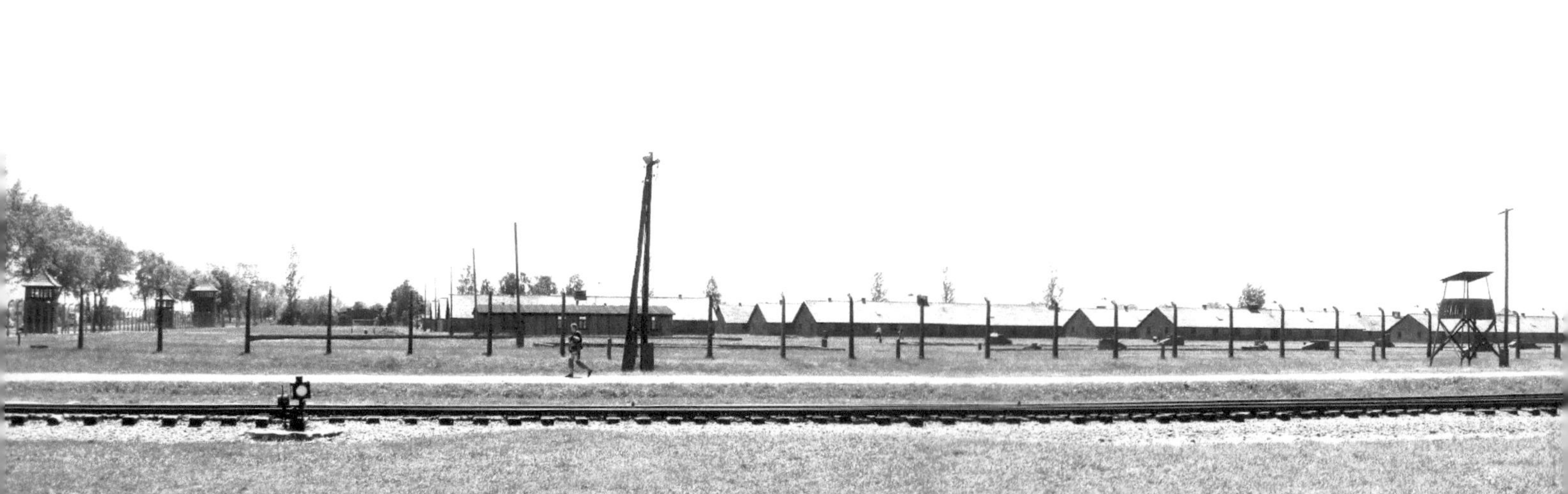

In the trees the birds are singing,
the pale sky brightens this morning,
a summer blue above me.

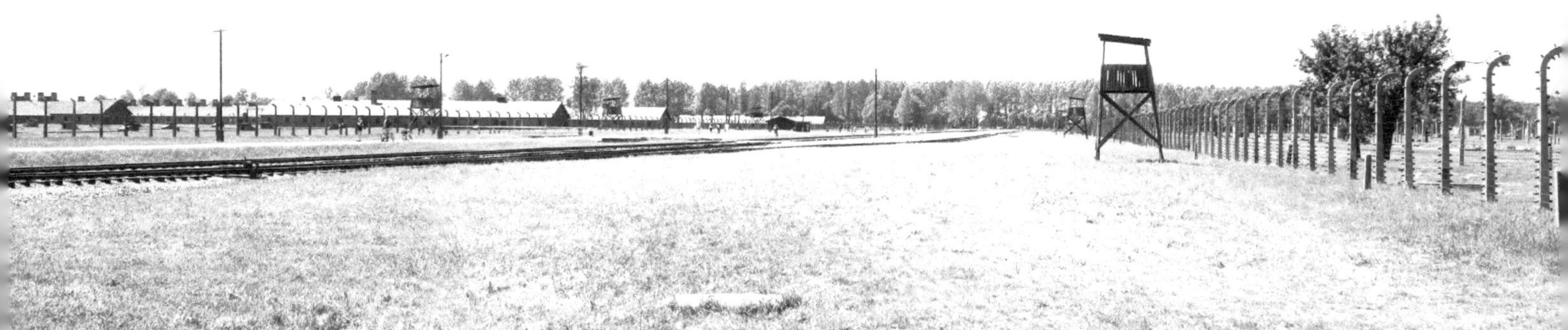

In early 1940 Rudolf Höss, a member of the SS, was appointed commandant of a new concentration camp in the recently occupied land of the Third Reich. On June 14th that same year, the first prisoners arrived[1] at Auschwitz. The camp was set up in an old Austro-Hungarian[2] army barracks, on the edge of the town of Oświęcim (Auschwitz in German). Auschwitz was initially a concentration camp[3] like those started in the 1930s Germany.

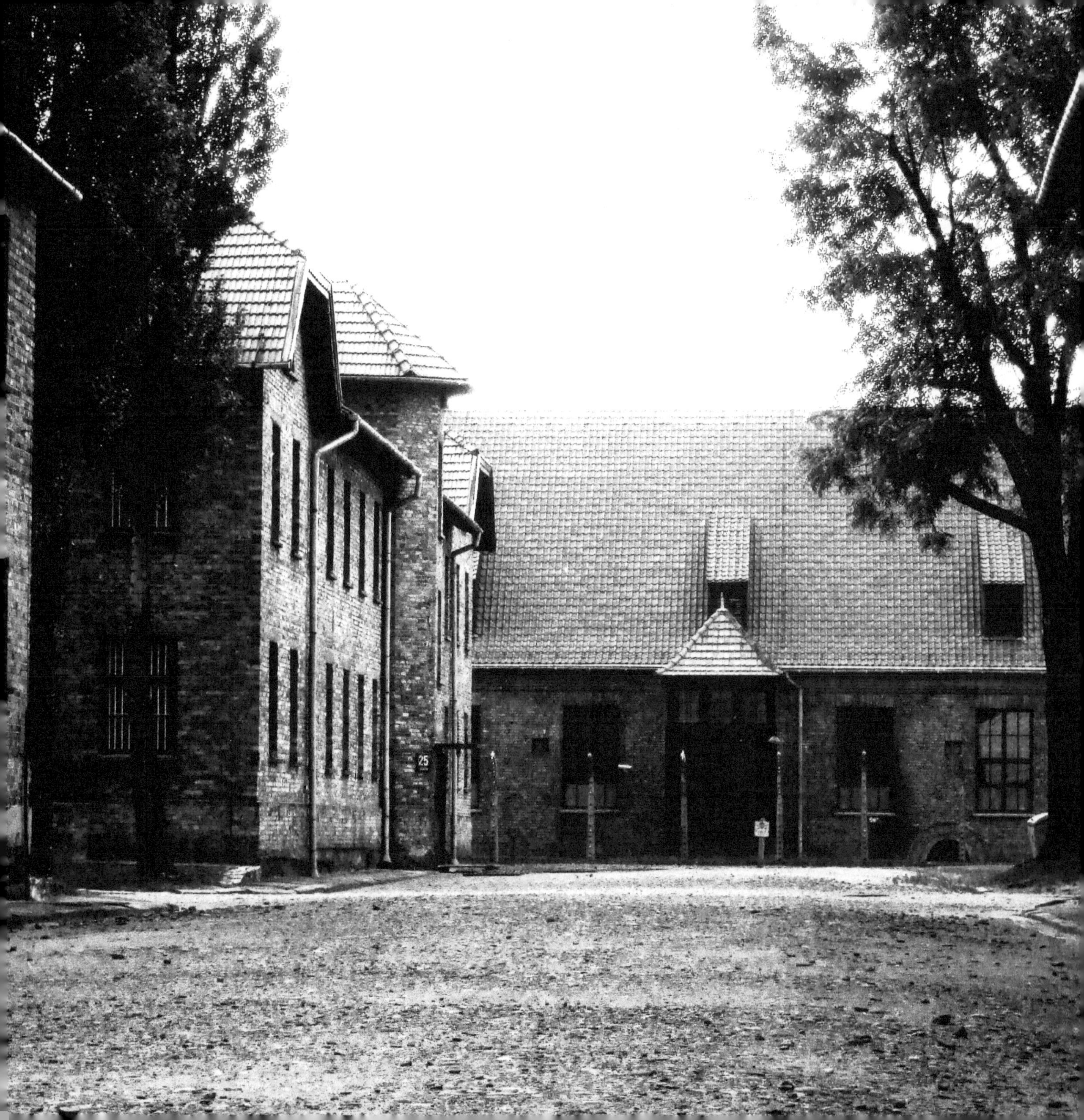
25

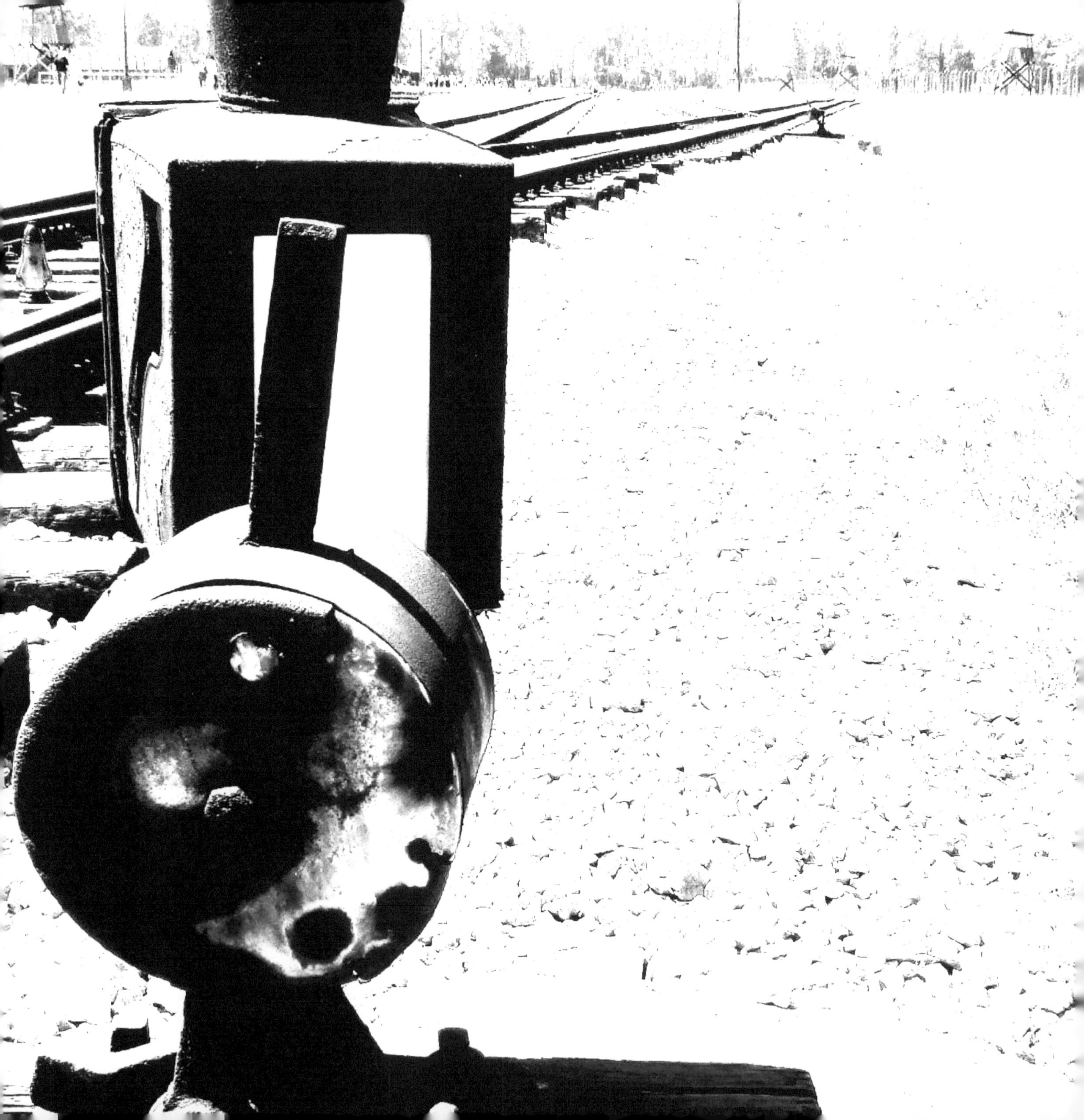

The dew traced grasses sparkle green,
these feelings could not be foreseen,
breezy fresh air surrounds me.

AT FIRST IT WAS THE POLES WHO WERE CONFINED THERE, IN ORDER TO RELIEVE LOCAL PRISONS THAT WERE OVER-CAPACITATED DUE TO MASS ARRESTS[1] BY THE OCCUPYING SS FORCES. SUBSEQUENTLY THOSE IMPRISONED THERE WERE THE SOVIET PRISONERS OF WAR, TAKEN FROM THE THIRD REICH'S EASTERN FRONT. THE GYPSIES CAME NEXT. THE POLES[2] INCLUDED THE ELITE, THE POLITICAL, CIVIC, AND SPIRITUAL LEADERS, MEMBERS OF THE INTELLIGENTSIA, THEIR CULTURAL AND SCIENTIFIC FIGURES, THE SOCIALLY REJECTED, AND THE MEMBERS OF THE RESISTANCE. IN A SELF-FULFILLING PHILOSOPHY, THE THIRD REICH BELIEVED THAT THE EASTERN RACES WERE INFERIOR TO THEIR OWN ARYAN[3] RACE, AND BY REMOVING THE INFLUENTIAL AND CULTURAL POLES FROM SOCIETY, THIS PHILOSOPHY BECAME APPARENT TO THEM.

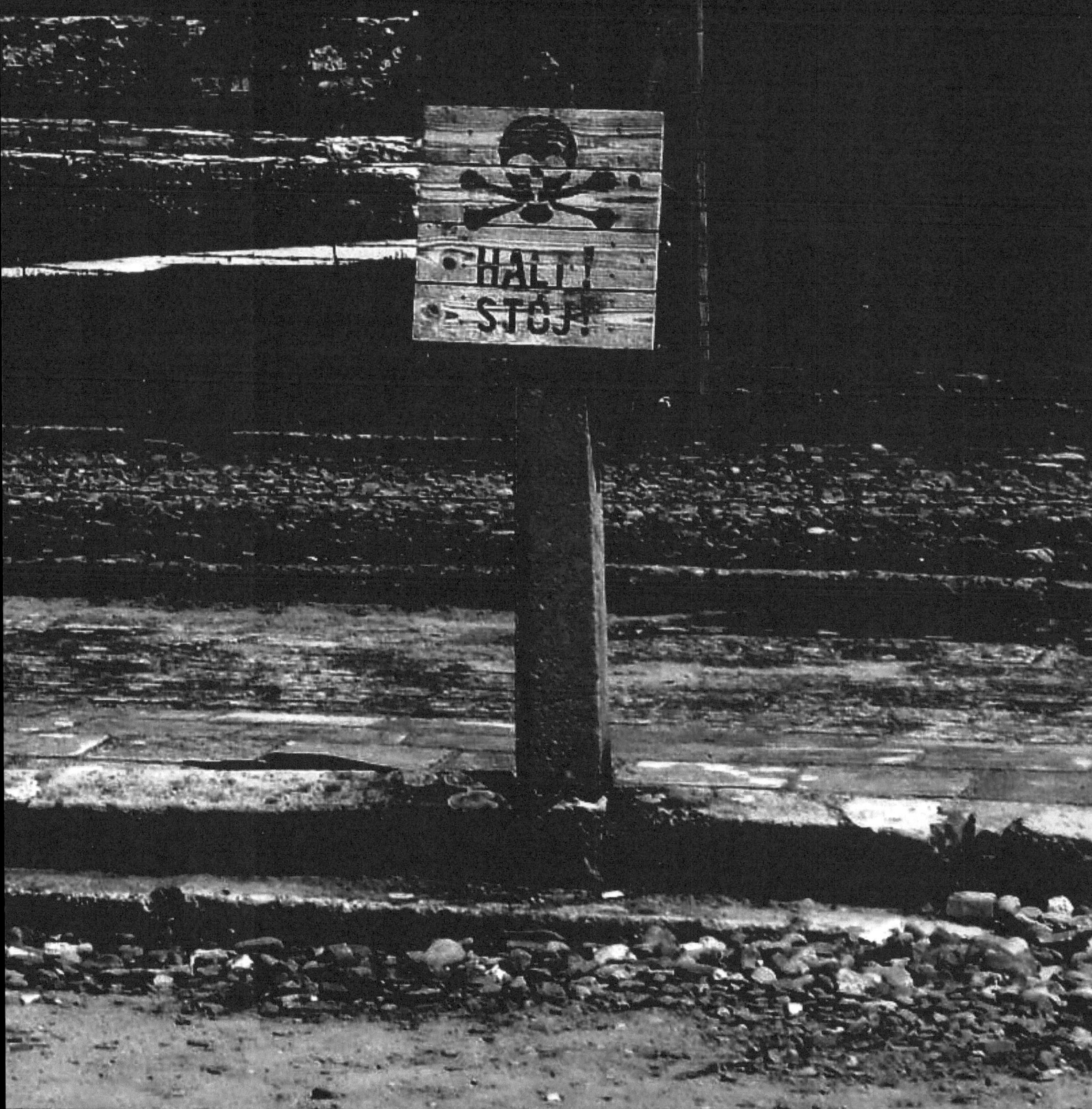
HALT!
STÓJ!

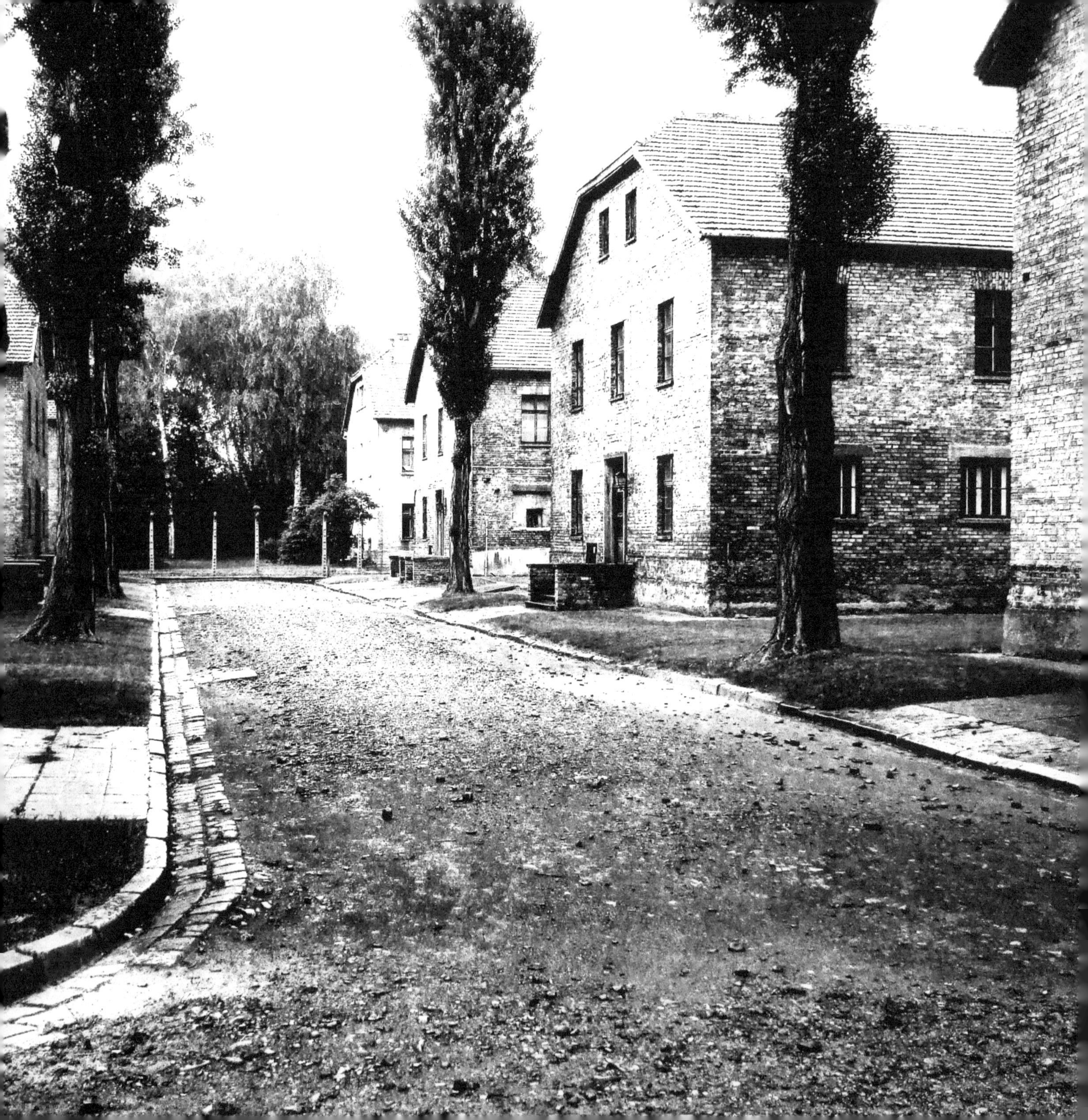

Lining the road are mature trees,
contrasting aged brick are the leaves
casting shadows, I pass by.

In 1941, Heinrich Himmler visited Auschwitz[1] and ordered Höss to expand the camp to include 100,000 Soviet POW's. The new camp was built three kilometers from Auschwitz I in a swampy area, in the town of Brzezinka (Birkenau in German). The Germans evicted the Poles from Oświęcim and Brzezinka in 1940 and 1941, destroying over 1,000 homes to build and expand the camp, opening Birkenau[2] in the spring of 1942. Increasing in scope and size, Auschwitz II–Birkenau and the Auschwitz III–Monowitz, were added to the initial Auschwitz I camp.

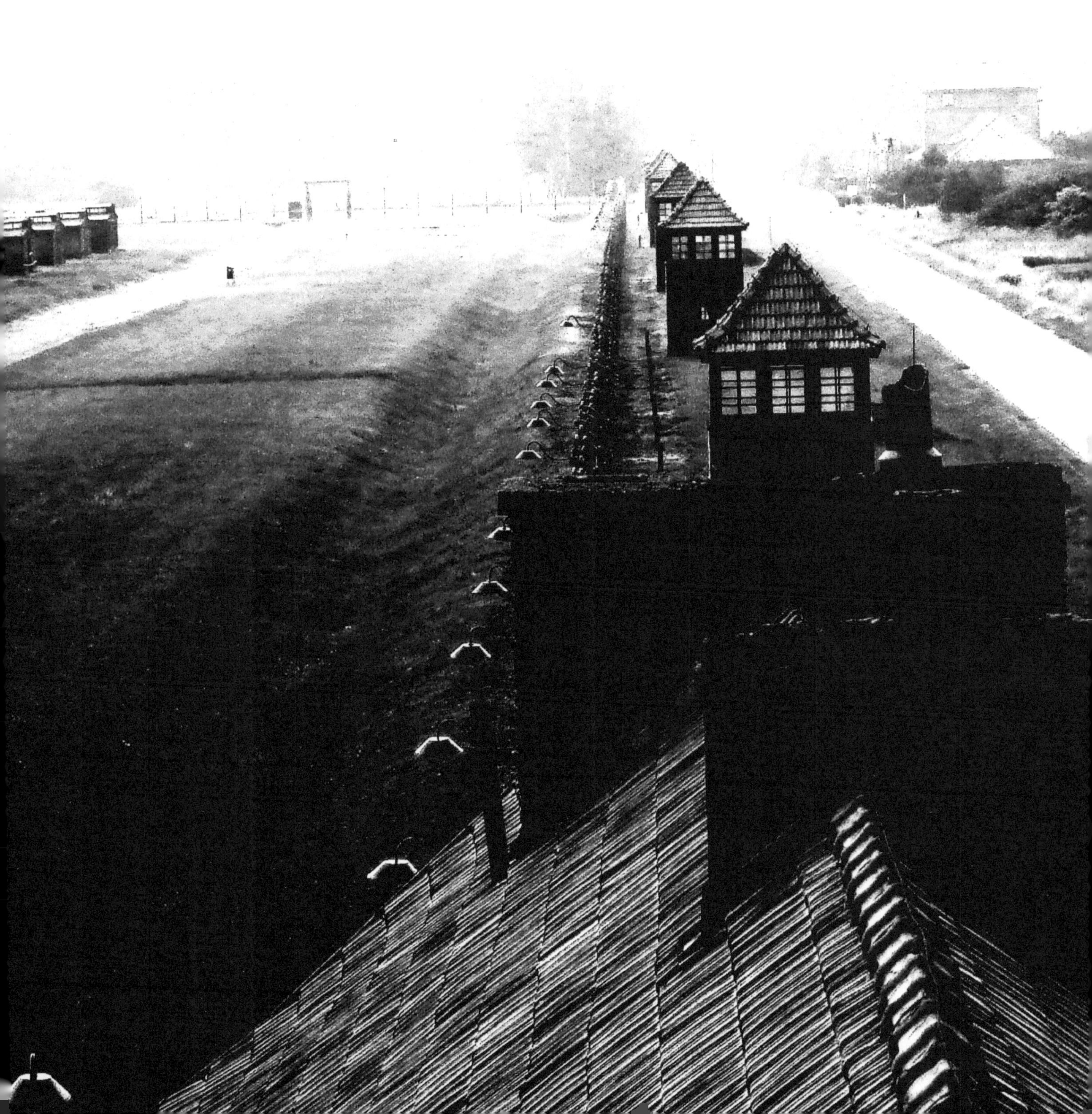

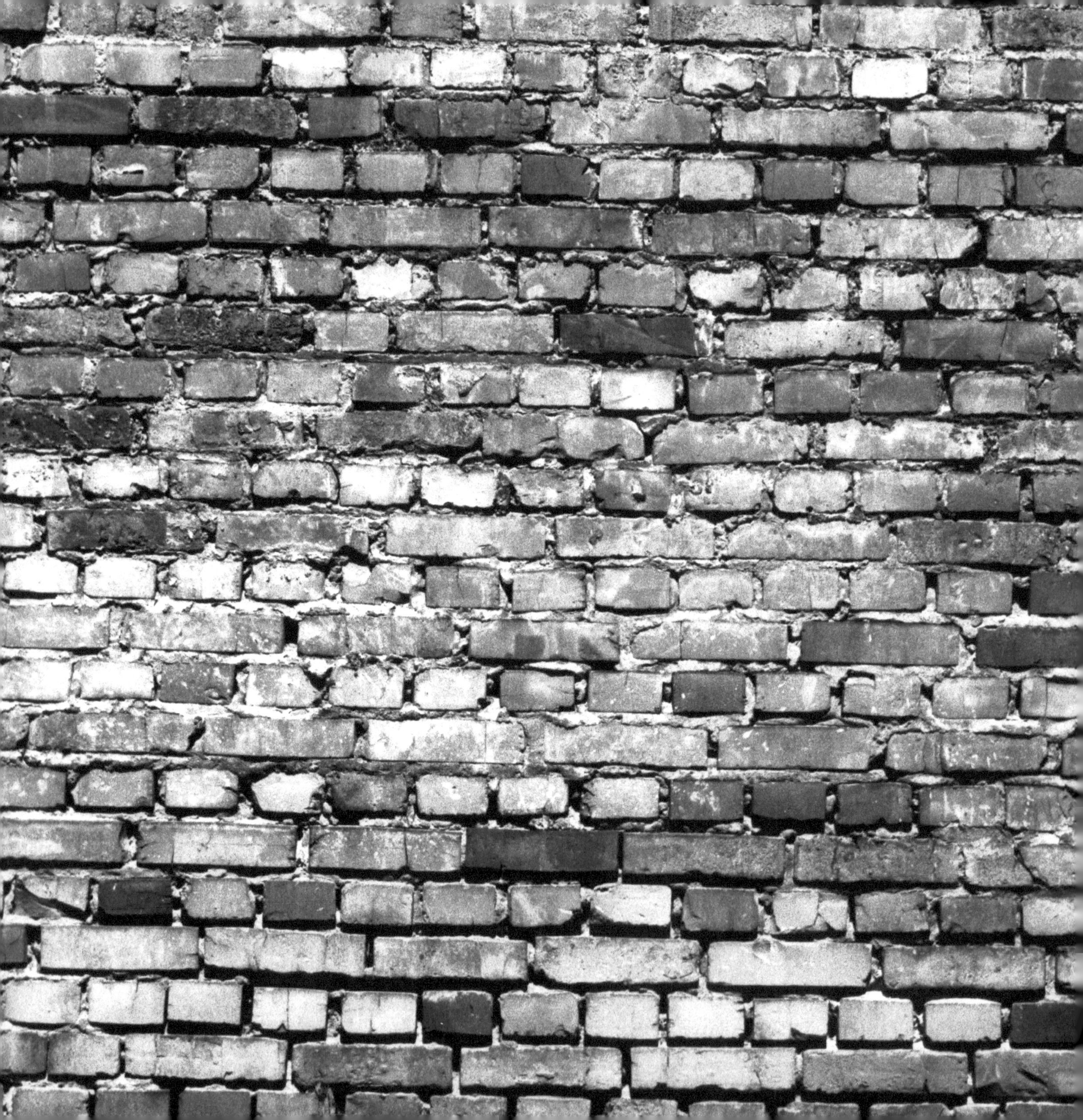

The weathered bricks sun warmed,
community here imagined,
living here, this place to die.

One of Höss's first gestures of his intentions at Auschwitz was to install a sign over the entrance that read in German "ARBEIT MACHT FREI" ("WORK BRINGS FREEDOM").[1] Within this philosophy, the concentration camp would provide a workforce that would not only sustain itself but become part of the economic engine of the Third Reich. With the decision to build the I.G. Farben rubber factory in nearby Buna, Auschwitz would help supply the raw materials and manpower to the company at a price. This vastly expanded and changed Himmler's and Höss's vision of Auschwitz as a place for agricultural research[2], into a place for industrial labor.

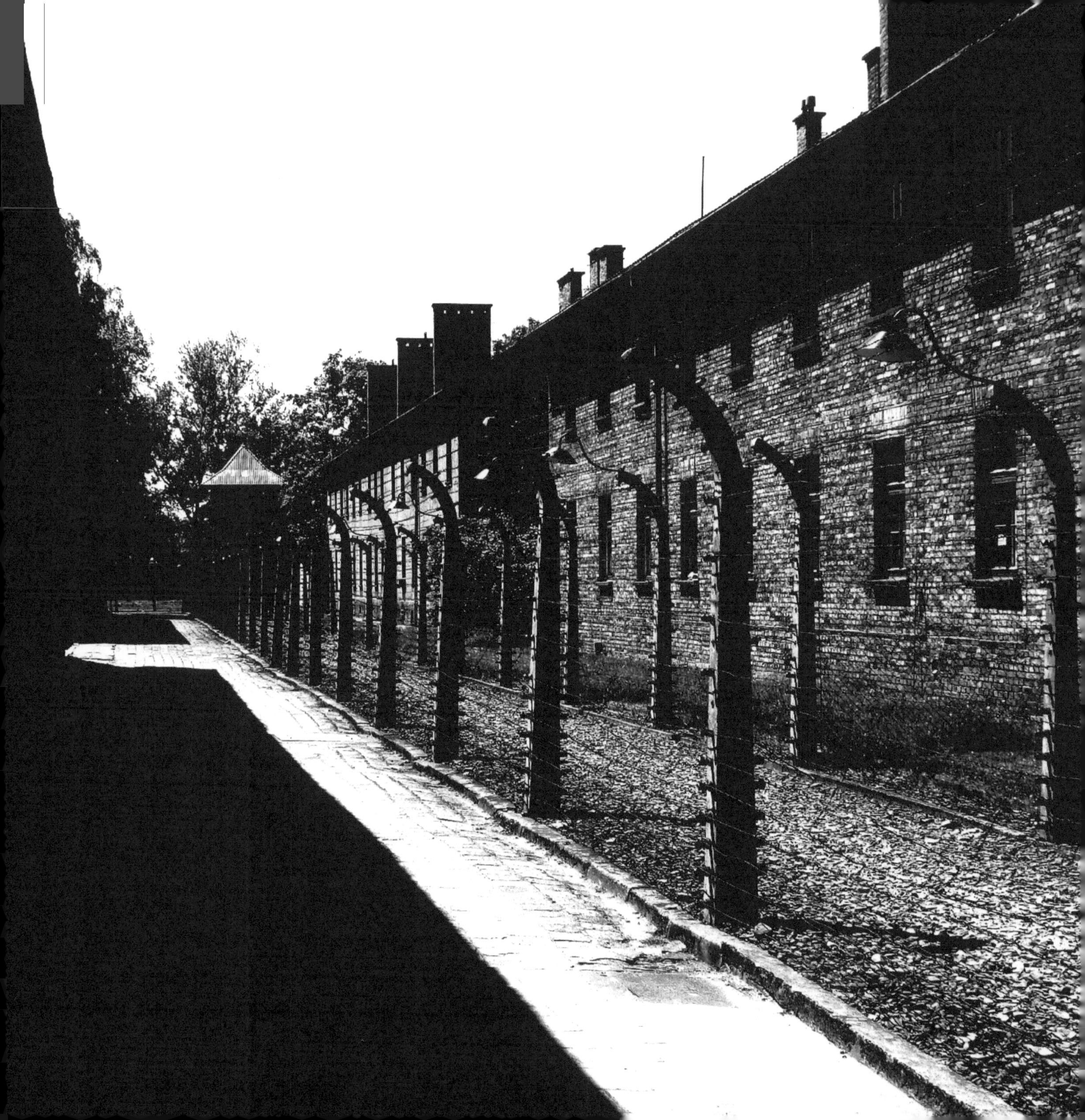

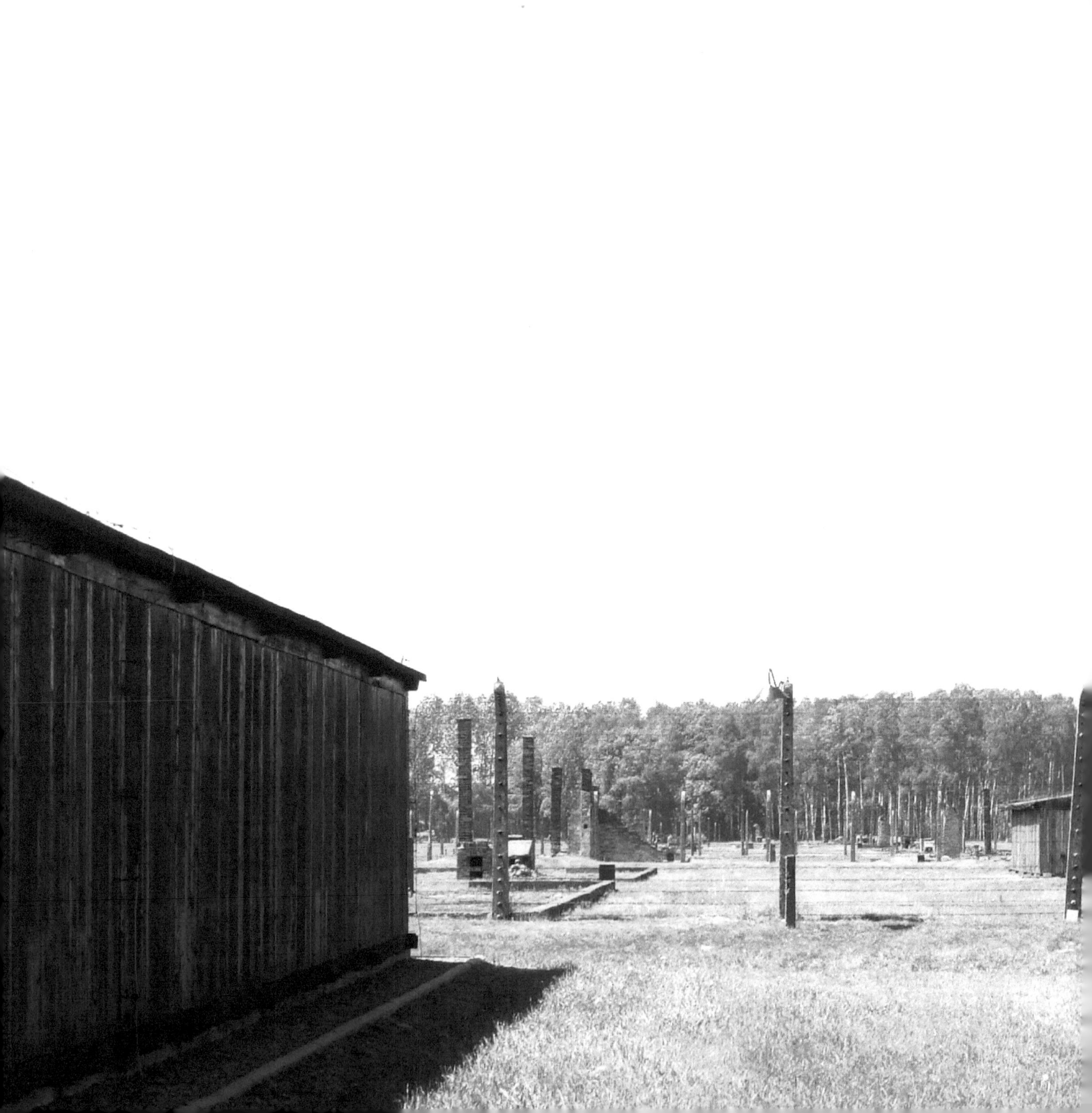

I had always known about it,
I just never knew about it,
realities of this place.

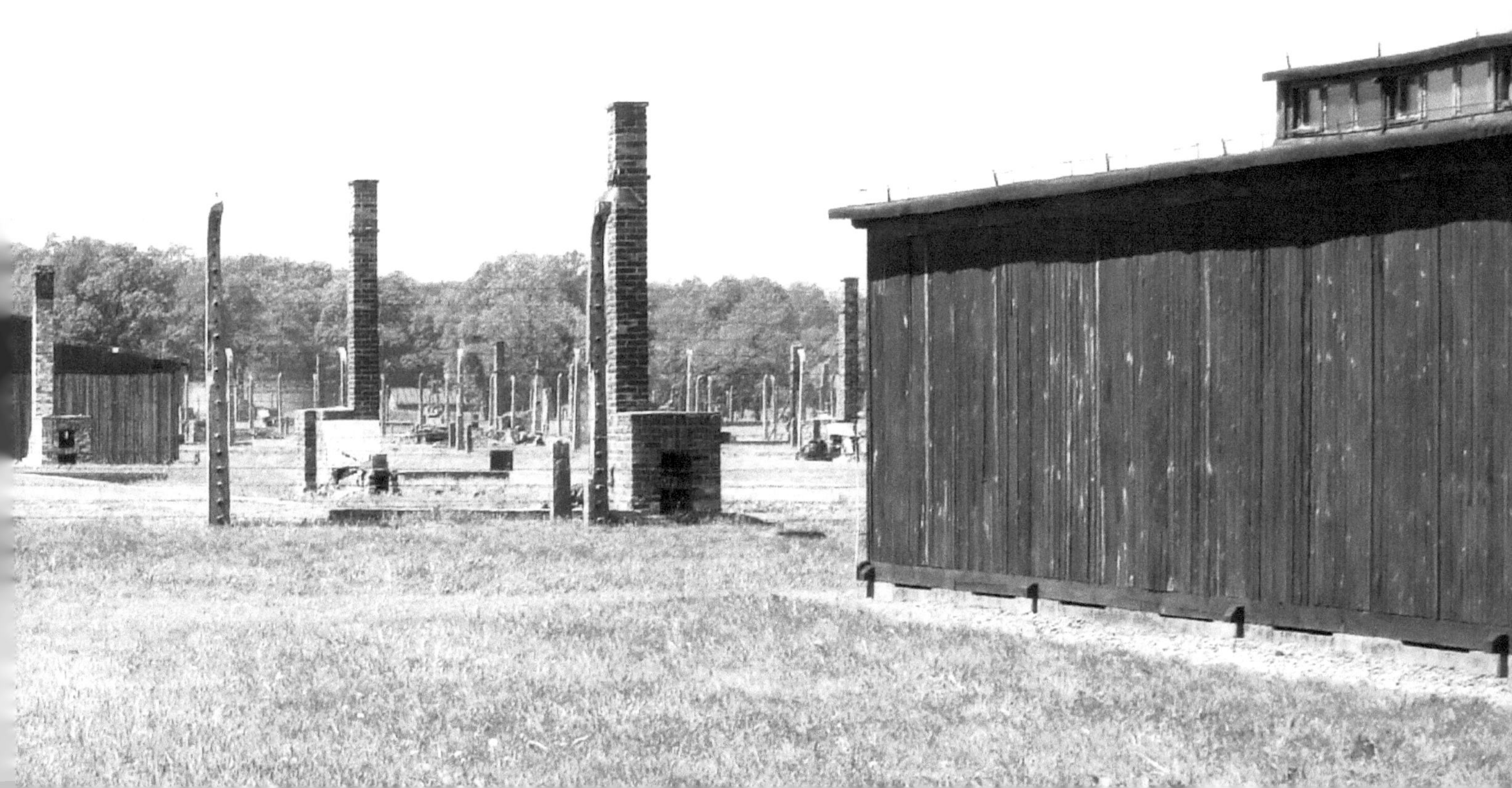

In the summer of 1941, the only method of mass killing in Auschwitz was shooting,[1] the same method used throughout the Third Reich. This was about to change. Death camps were being set up across Poland with the plan to use a new method of mass killing: gassing. First, Chełmno in 1941; then in rapid succession[2] in 1942, Bełżec, Sobibór, and Treblinka. These death camps were set up as Operation Reinhard to begin the "final solution," the total removal of the Jewish race from Europe by extermination. The creation of Jewish ghettoes was the failed solution.

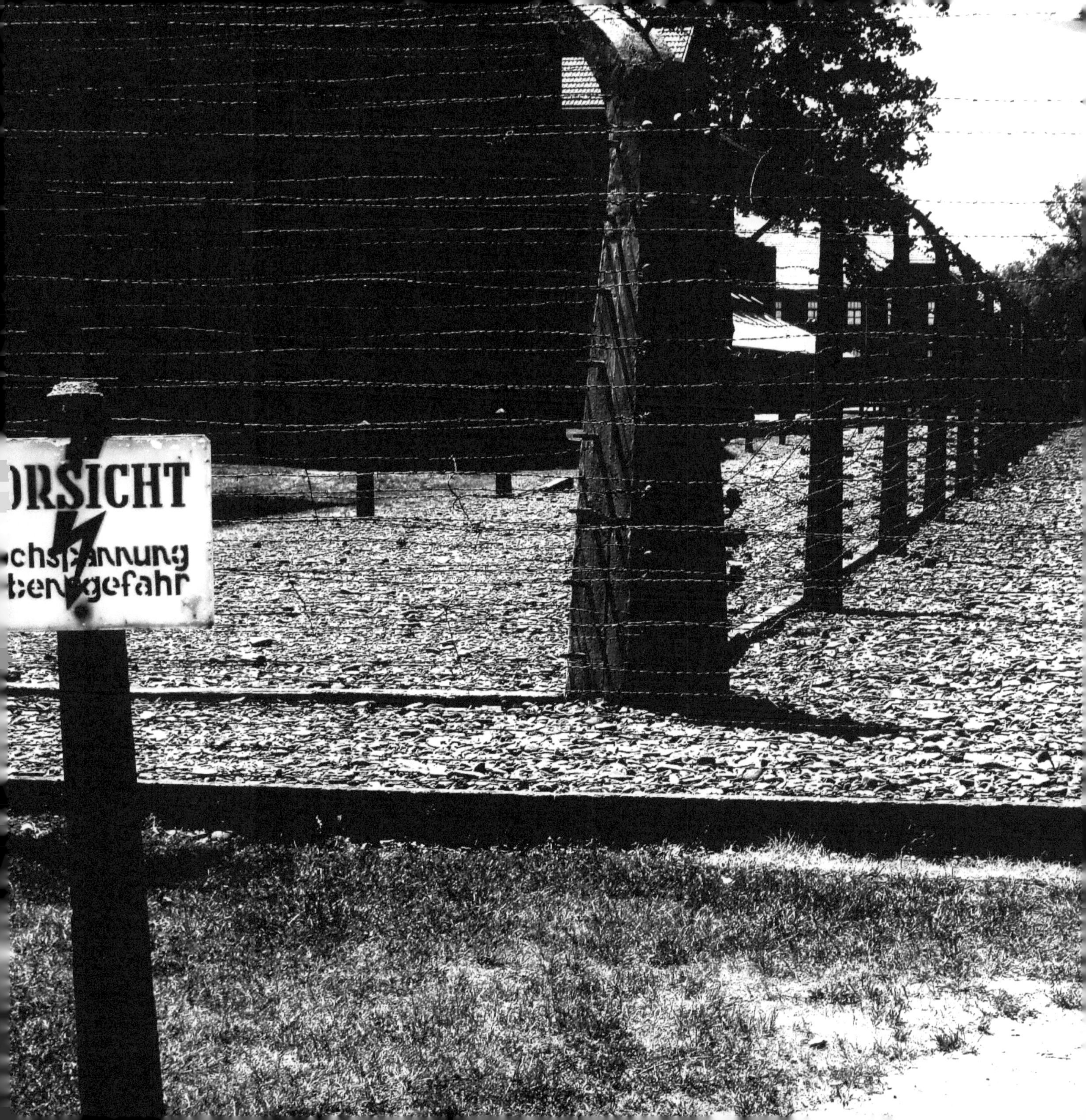
ORSICHT
chspannung
bensgefahr

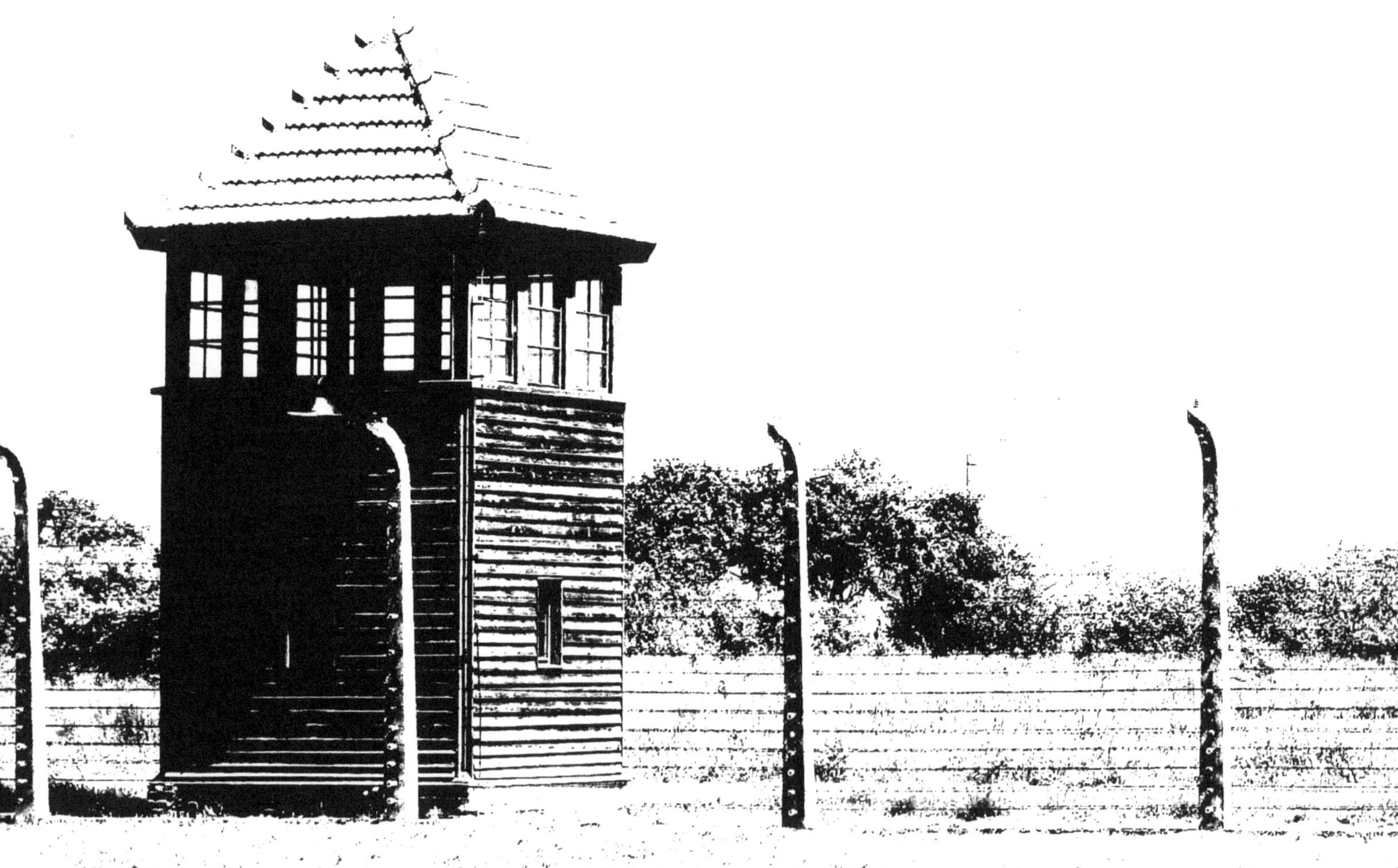

Saddened by the unaffected,
escape with normal actions tried,
posing regardless of place.

Auschwitz, under Höss's leadership, was developing new methods of killing as well. In the autumn of 1941 experiments were being carried out using Zyklon B, hydrogen cyanide and prussic acid, a rat poison. A group of Soviet prisoners[1] were gassed in the basement of Block 11. For SS convenience the trial gassings were eventually moved to the crematorium at the edge of Auschwitz I where newly arriving Jews from the surrounding region of Upper Silesia or those deemed unfit for work[2] were among those gassed. Revving motorcycles were used outside of the crematorium to mask the sounds of death coming from the victims inside, without success.[3]

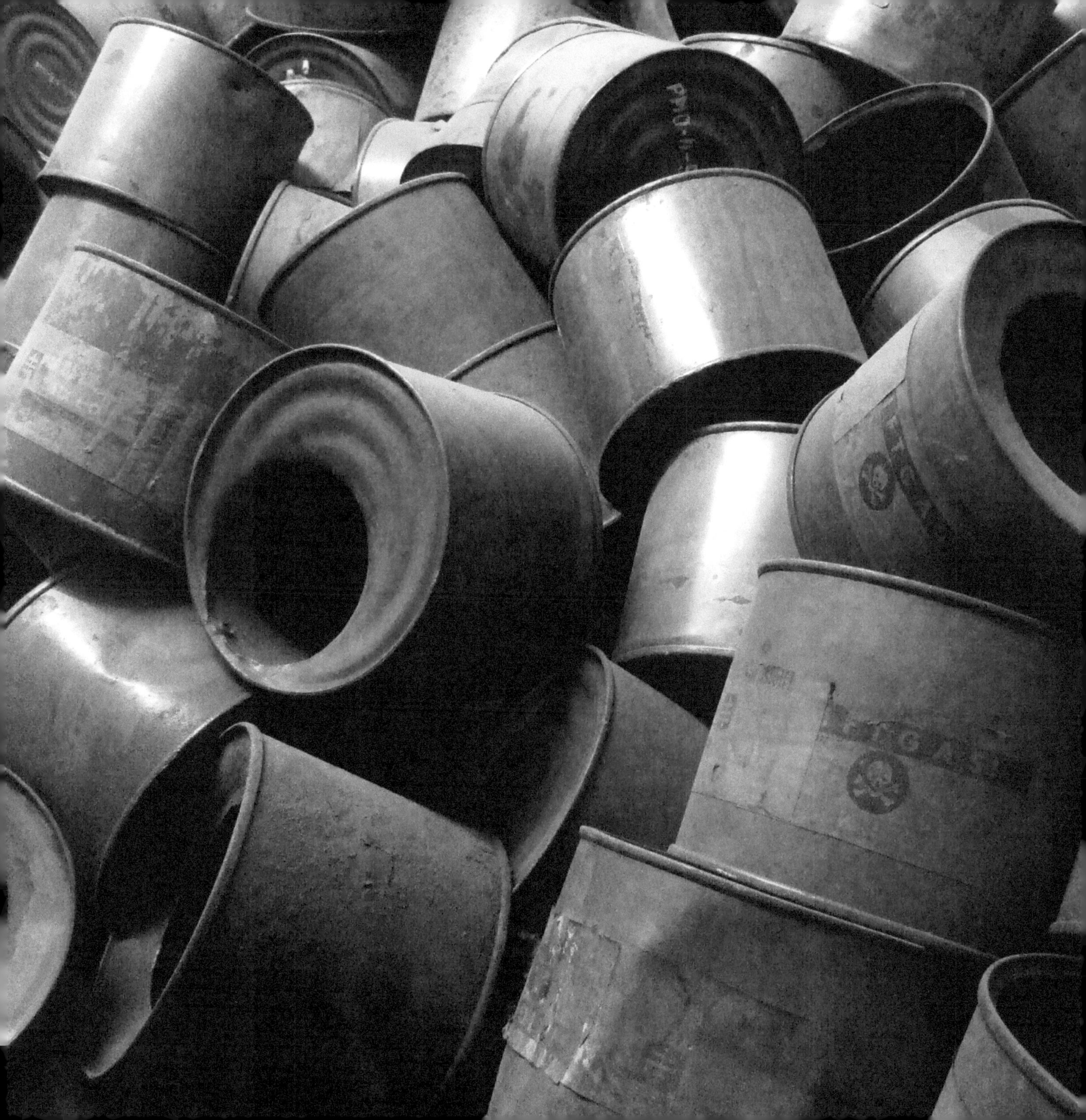

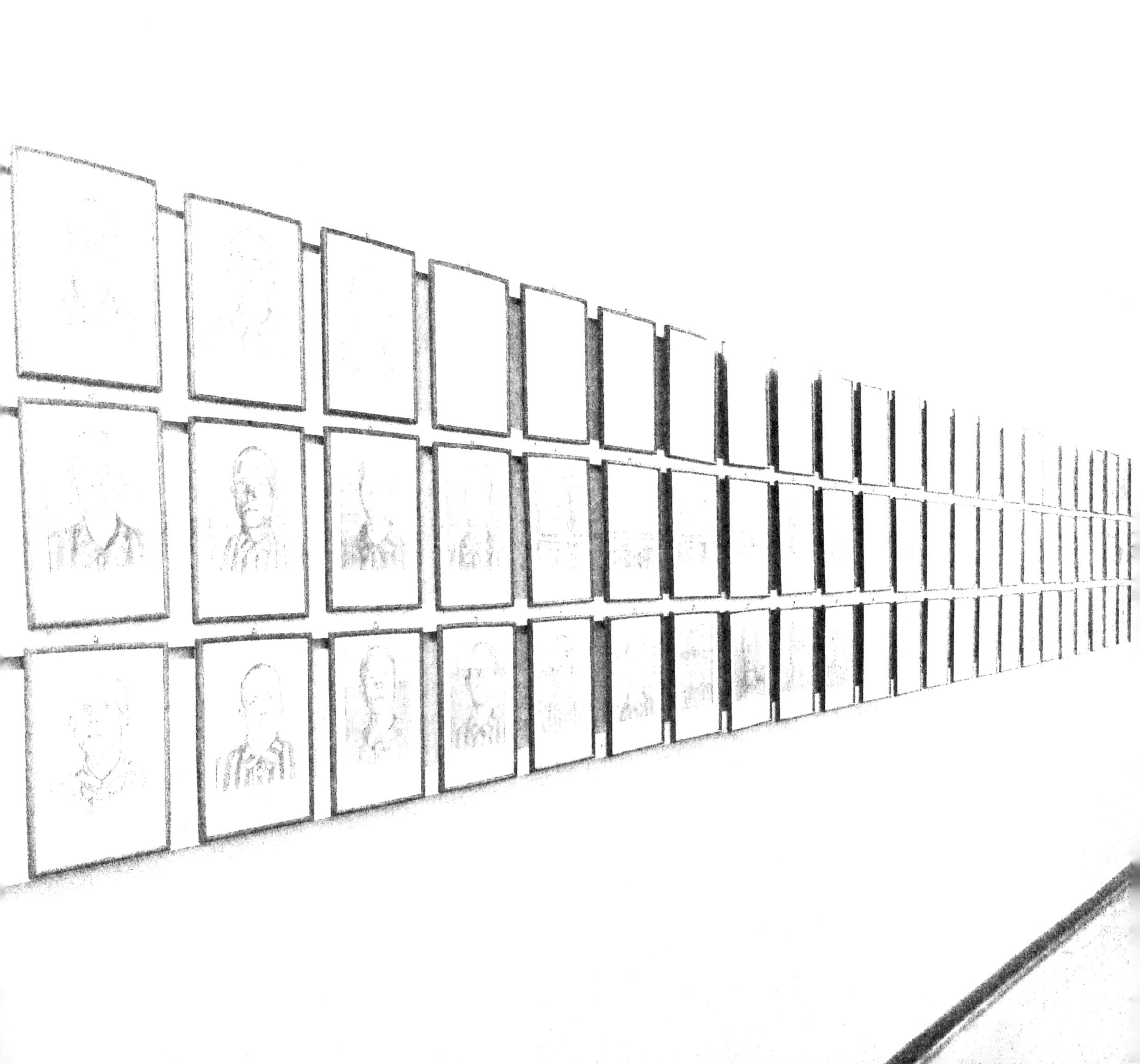

Face to face to early prisoned,
knowing they must have succumbed.
I know not reality.

By the end of 1942, 1.4 million Jews had been killed in the death camps outside of Auschwitz.[1] In that same year, the killings in the gas chambers had moved to Bunker 1, and 2: "The Little Red House," and "The Little White House." Here as many as 175,000 Jews were killed that year.[2] The SS soon realized, that it was easier to trick the victims into the gas chambers, by suggesting that they were going to a room to be disinfected and that they would be able to gather their belongings when finished.[3] In this way the SS and the Sonderkommando (German for "special unit," referring to the prisoners put in charge of disposing of the bodies) were able to separate the victims from their cloths and belongings easier.

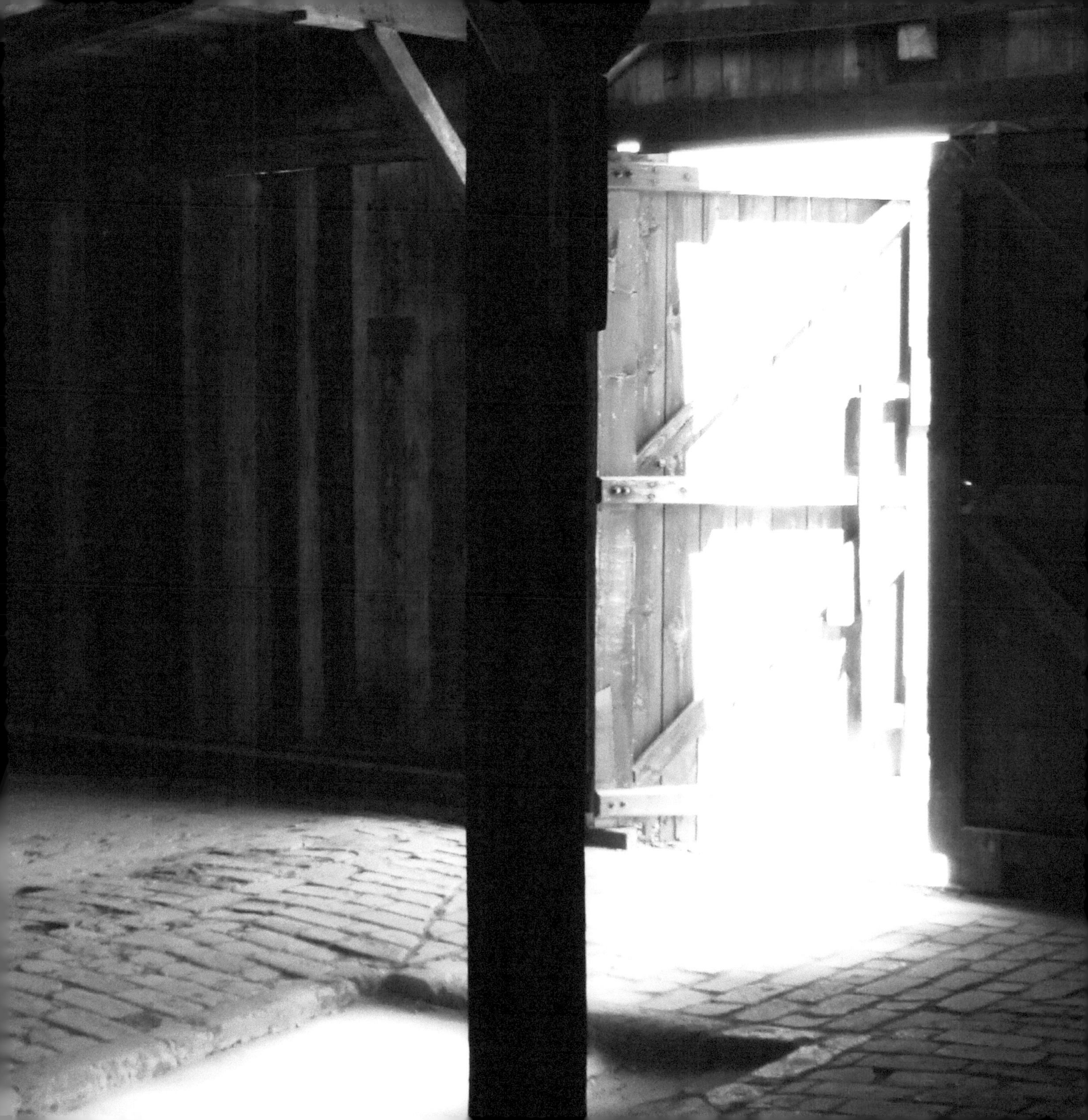

My mind no longer allows me to think.
Nothing
We move on.

At the beginning, prisoners at Auschwitz were photographed for identification. Due to starvation disease and abuse, it became increasingly difficult for the camp staff to identify the victims once they had been killed or died. To ease the difficulty of identification, the new prisoners were tattooed[1] with an identification number. This number became their name, striping them of their last bit of dignity. However, the majority of those arriving did not get a tattoo; because they were sent to immediate death[2] in the gas chambers.

Auschwitz I, held between 15,000 and 20,000 prisoners
Auschwitz II-Birkenau, held 90,000 in 1944

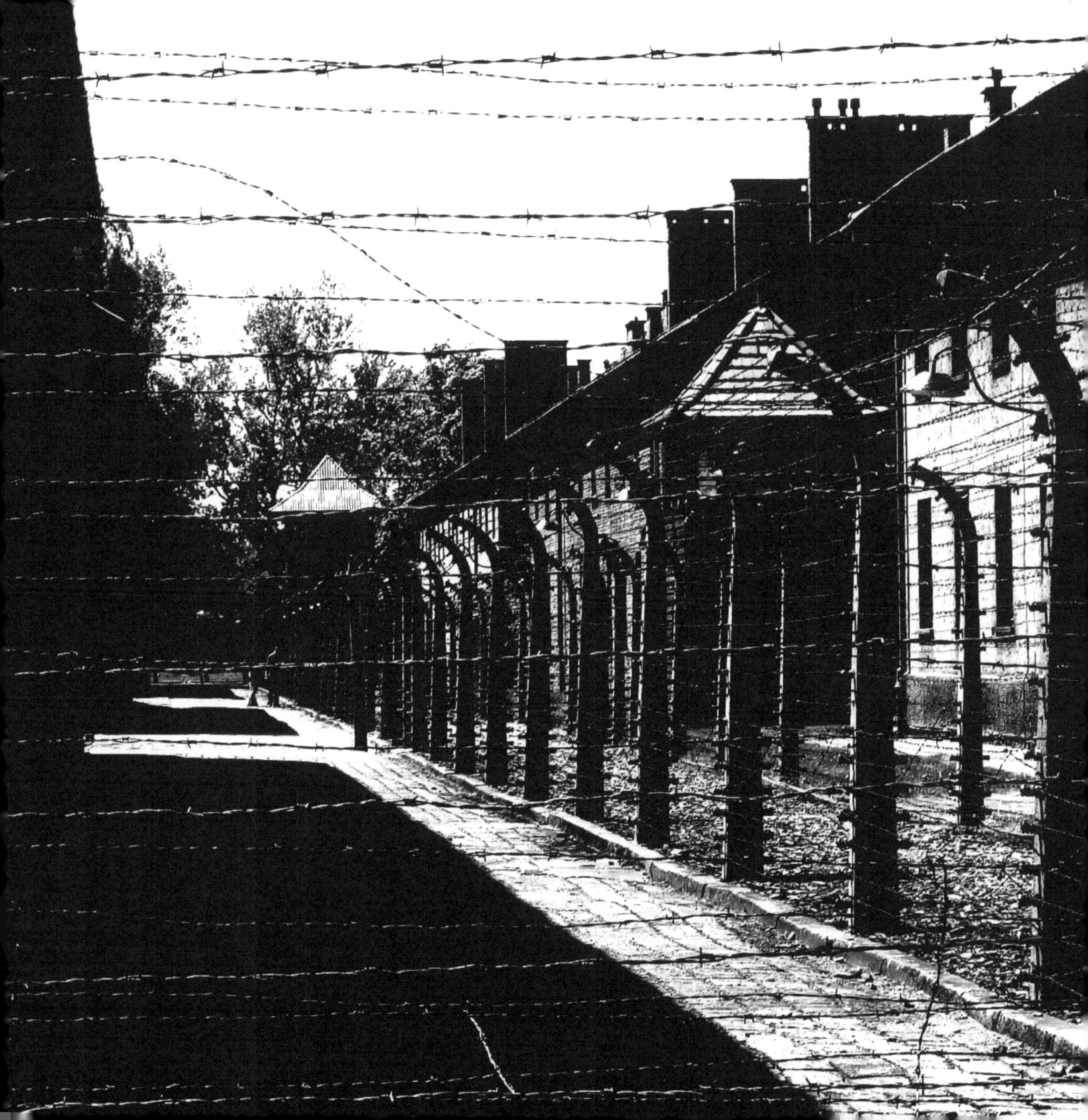

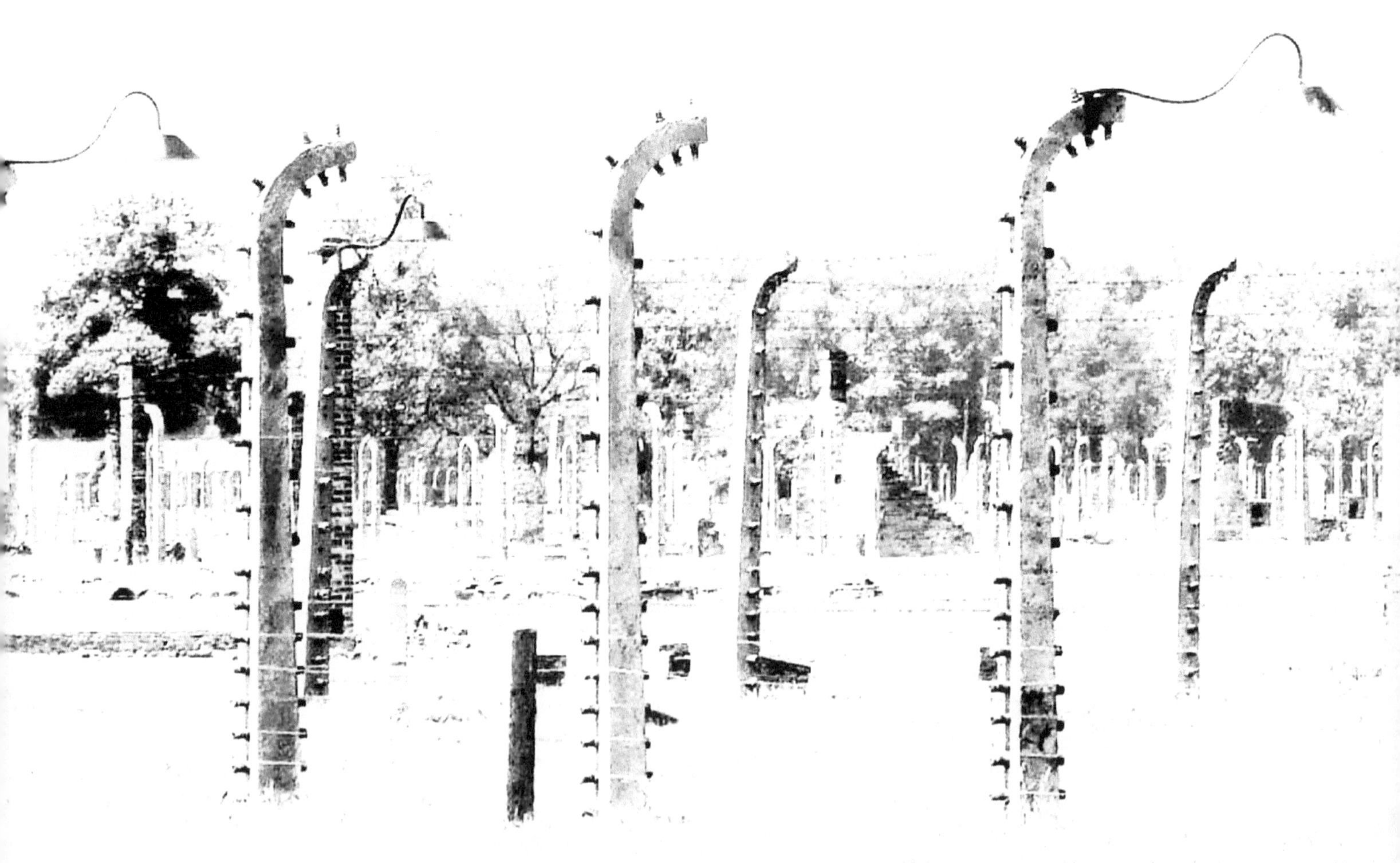

As Catholic, I am shame filled,
shameful, afar I could not understand.
Were they not my people too?

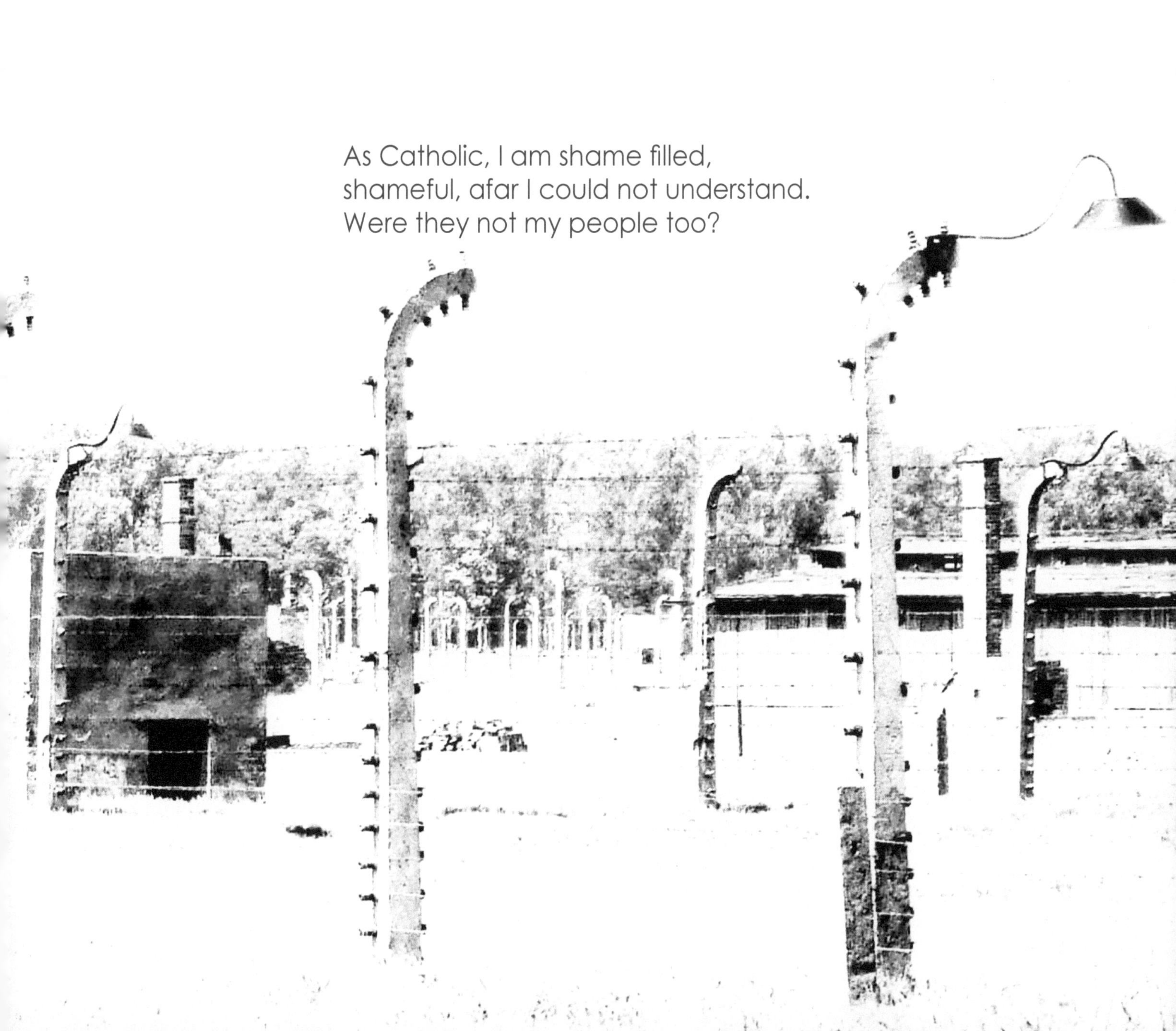

A Polish sergeant (imprisoned for involvement in the Jewish resistance) was chosen in a selection for retribution for an escaped prisoner from his block. This man was selected to die of starvation in the basement of Block 11 along with 9 others. When he pleaded for his life because he had a family, Father Maksymilian Kolbe a Polish Roman Catholic priest asked if he could be sentenced in his place. The Kapos (block leaders) agreed. After two weeks of starvation in a small cell[1] with only a small hole for air, Father Kolbe and 3 remaining prisoners were killed by lethal injection. The saved man survived the Holocaust. In 1982 Polish Pope John Paul II canonized the priest as Saint Maksymilian Kolbe.

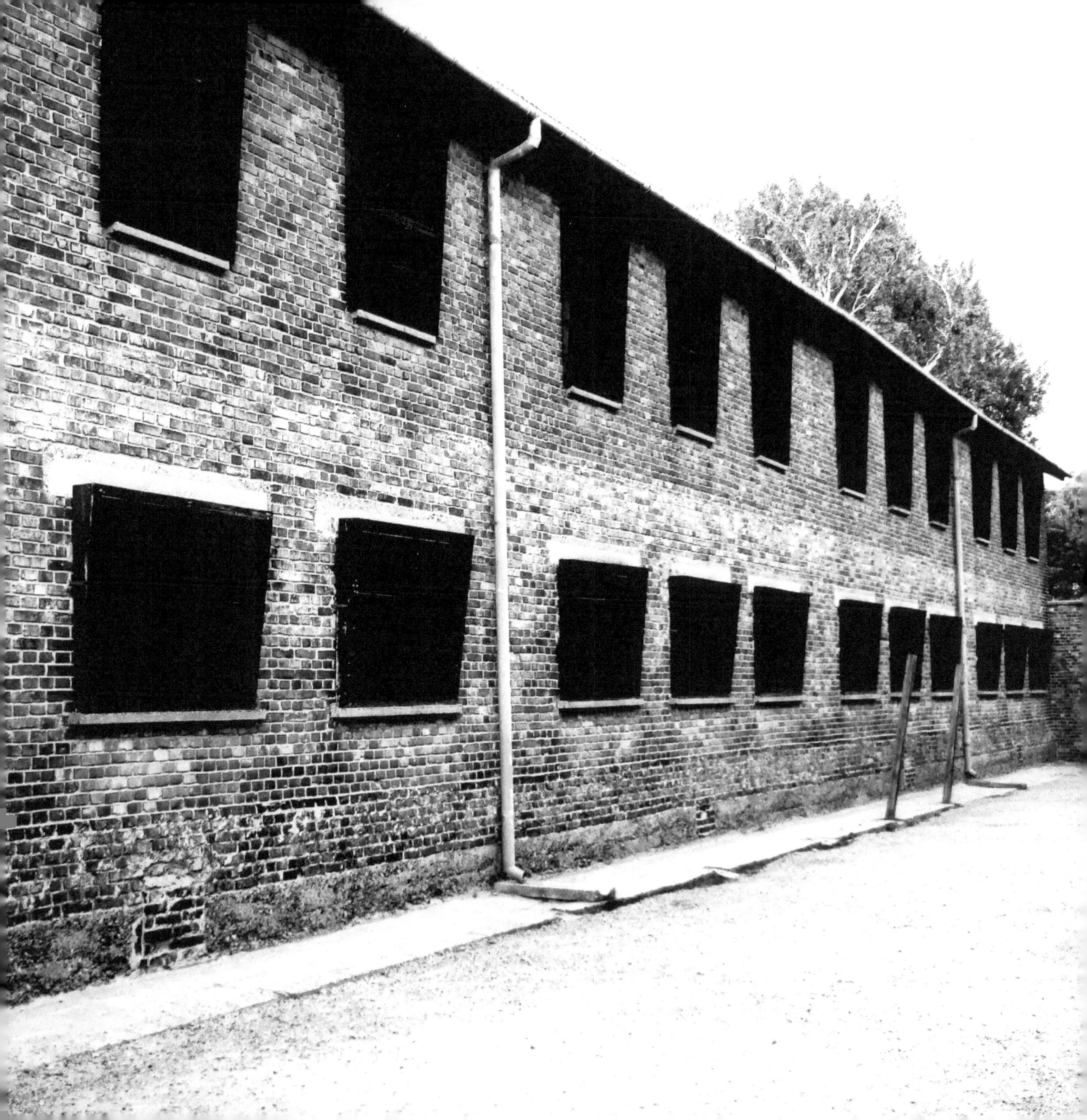

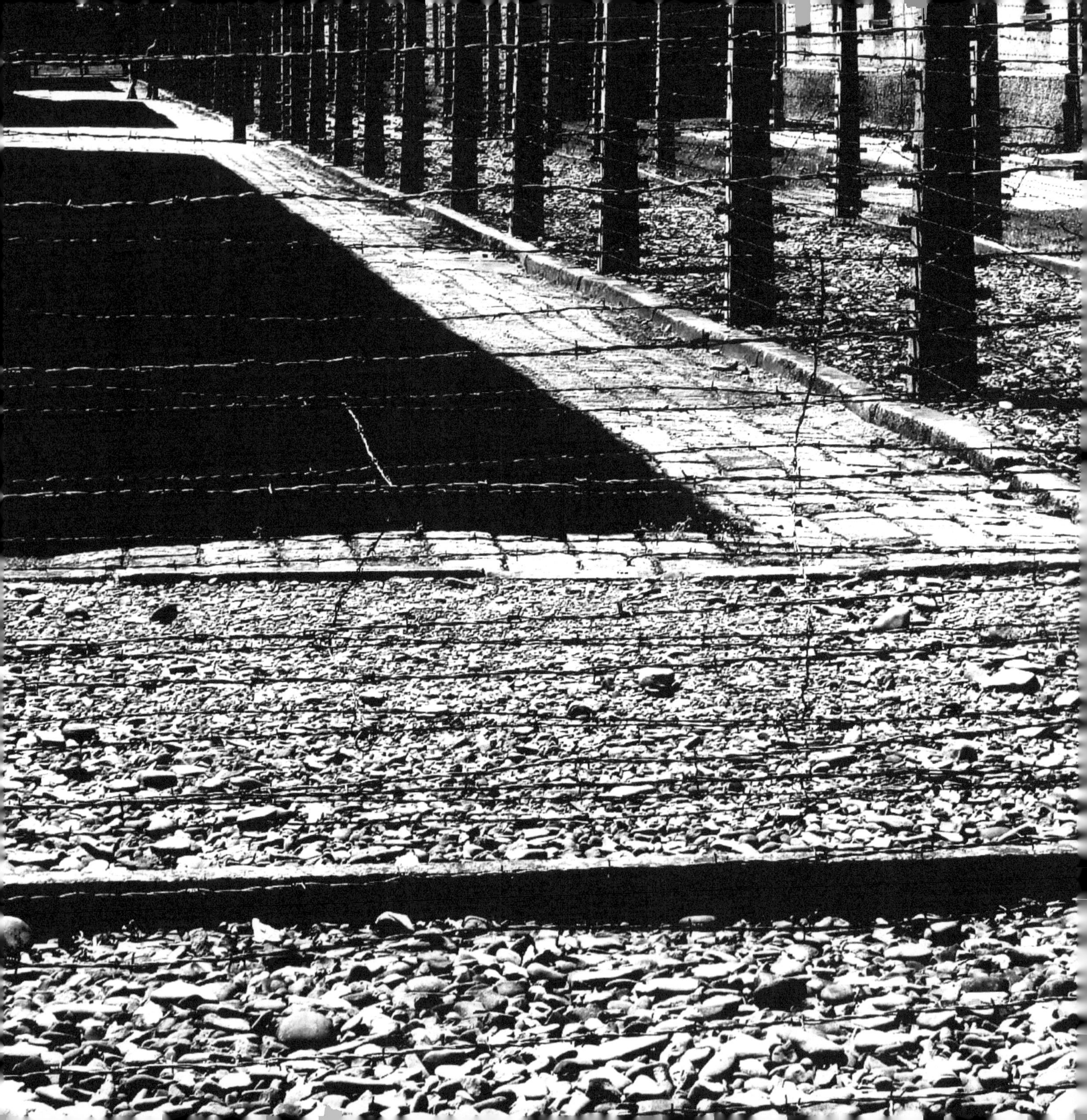

Once again my mind is numbed,
for all those who succumbed,
I hold my breath, in stale air.

Arrival at Auschwitz was not the beginning of the problems for many Jews. After increasing persecution, Jews were rounded up in their communities and sent to the ghettoes where many starved to death. Then they were selected for the "final solution" and put in cattle cars with no room to sit and little food or water.[1] The lucky ones would find themselves after (sometimes) a week of travel on a rail platform; "the ramp" facing an SS doctor[2] who would signal them left or right. Death or extended life awaited those still alive. Families were broken up, mothers screaming for their children, wandering children looking for lost parents, and people unable to cry. These Jews came from near and far: 438,000 from Hungary; 300,000 from Poland; 69,114 from France; 60,085 from the Netherlands; 55,000 from Greece; 46,099 from Czechoslovakia and Moravia; 23,000 from Germany and Austria; 26,661 from Slovakia; 24,906 from Belgium; 10,000 from Yugoslavia; and 7,422 from Italy. Non-Jews included: 70,000 political prisoners from Poland; more than 23,000 Gypsies; 10,000 Soviet prisoners of war; hundreds of Jehovah's Witnesses; the socially rejected; and some for no reason[3] at all.

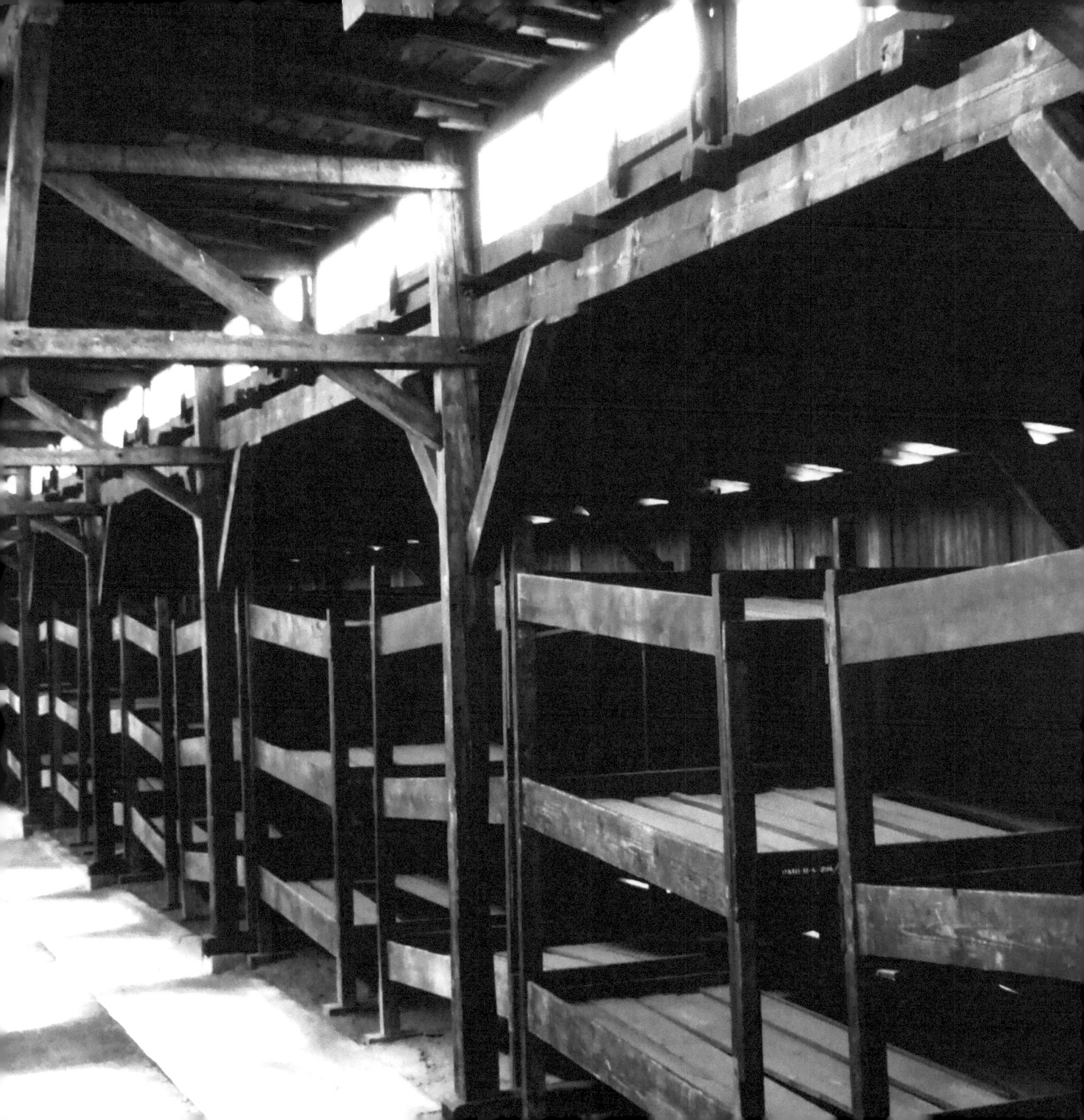

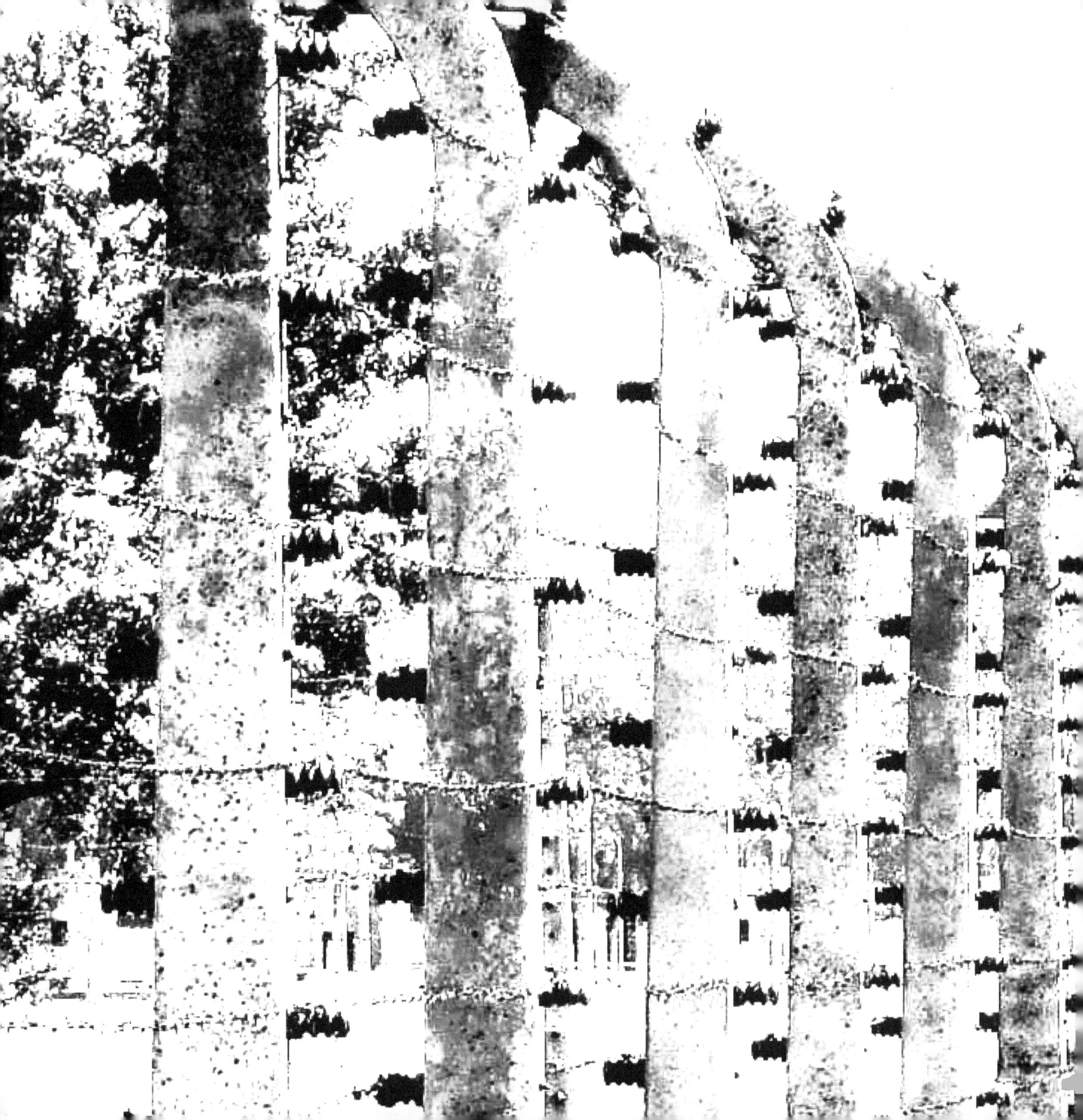

My body tired from the strain,
not wanting to deal with the pain,
I yearn for an end.

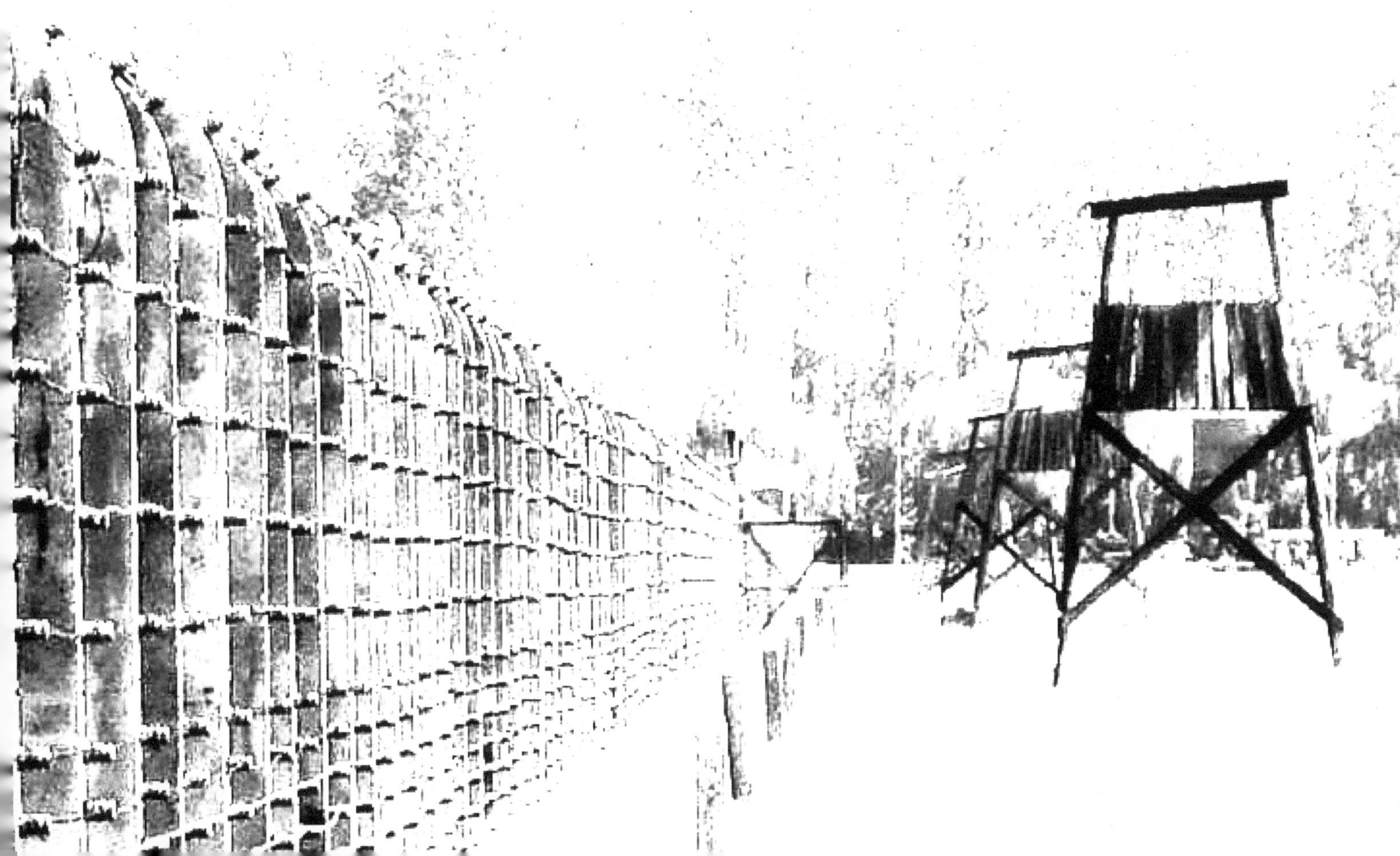

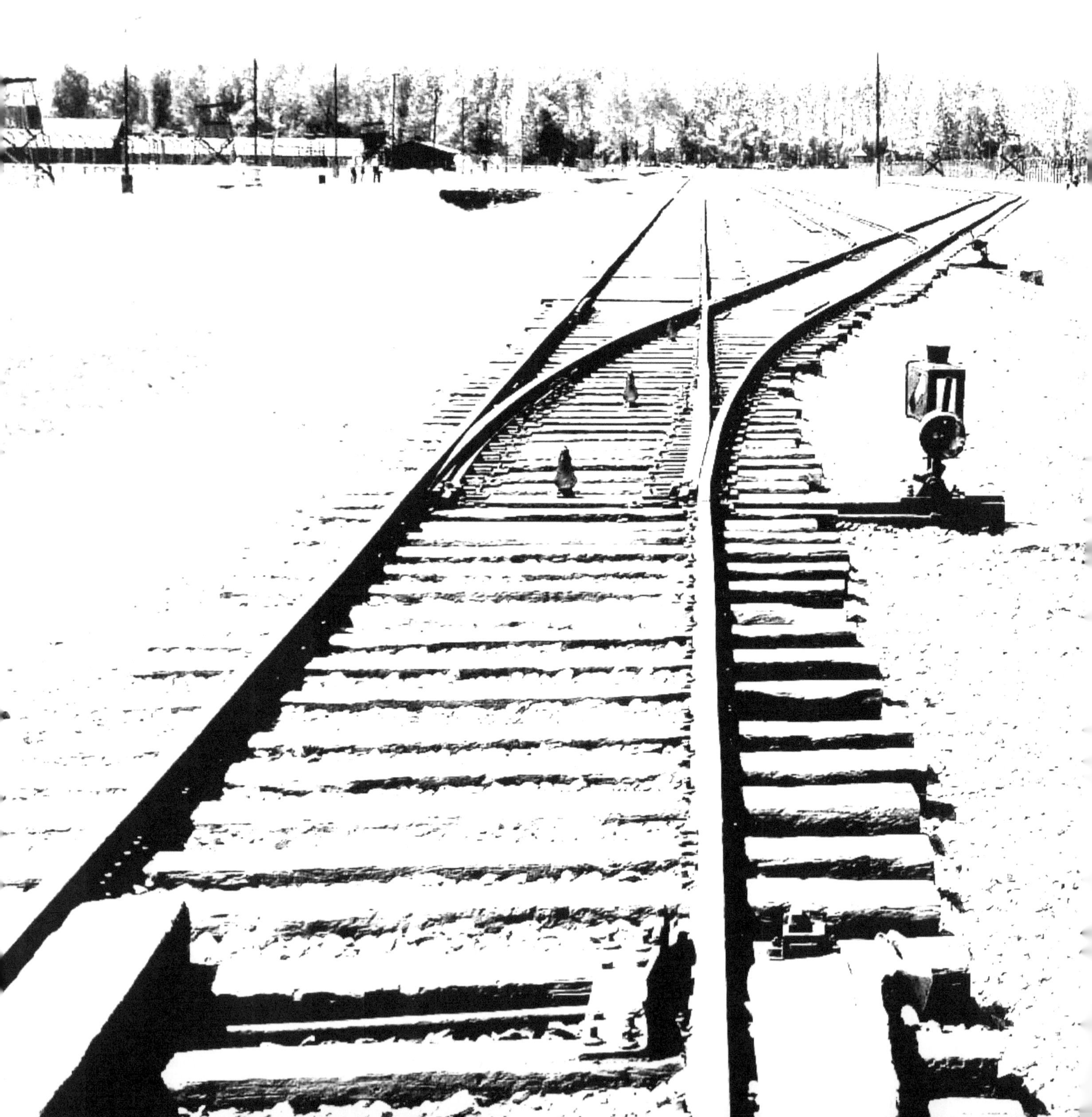

It was impossible to survive the harsh environment of Auschwitz. Poor nutrition, hard labor, exposure to the elements, and filthy living conditions contributed[1] to high death rates. Those who did not die "naturally" were chosen in the many selections to be sent to the "chimney," due to their poor visual health.[2] To survive, one needed a place of privilege to get better food, clothing, work conditions, and luck to stay in those positions. Survivors attest to many instances of good fortune[3] that allowed them to survive. Of the estimated 1,300,000 people to enter Auschwitz only 200,000 survived the war.[4]

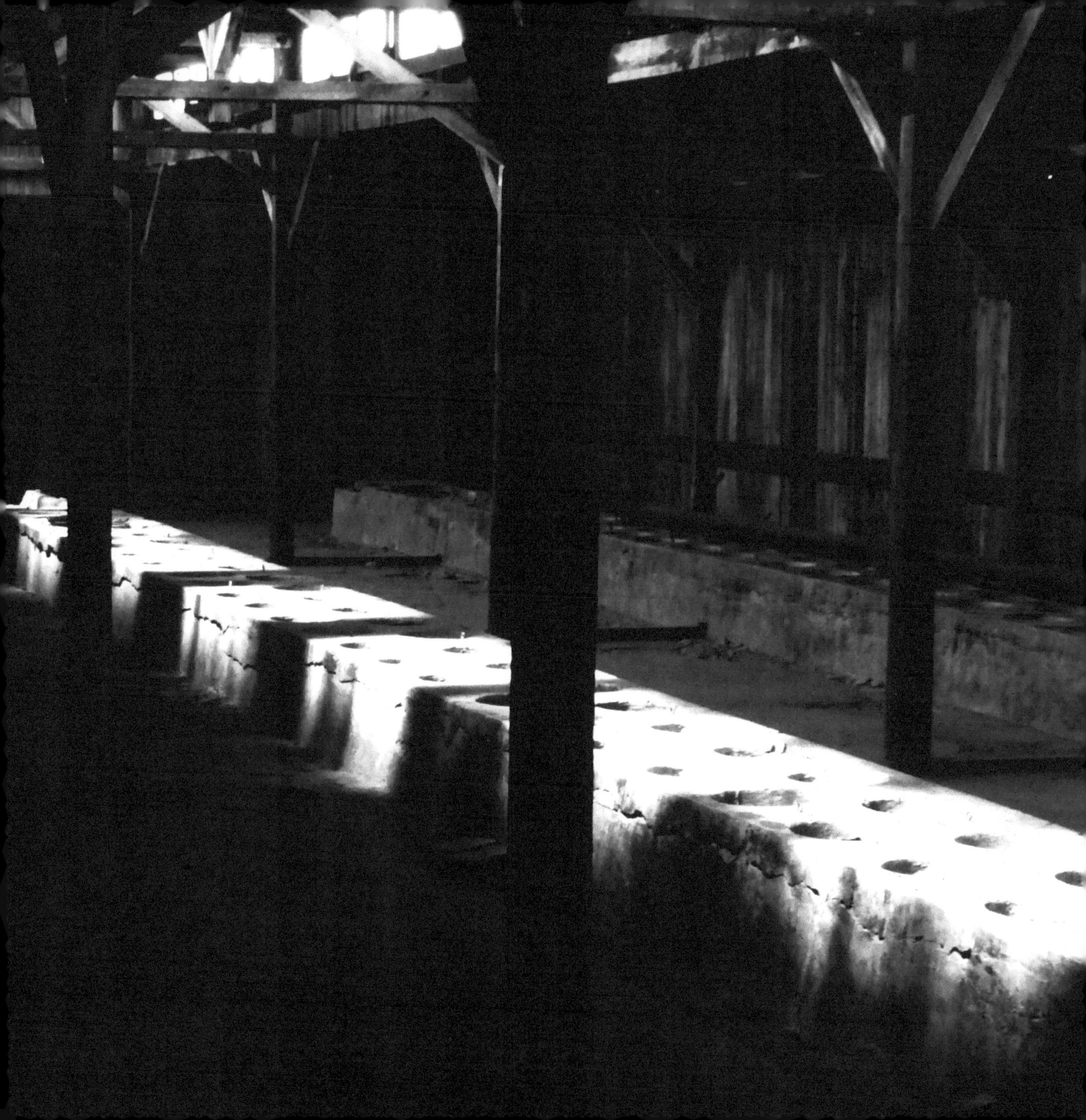

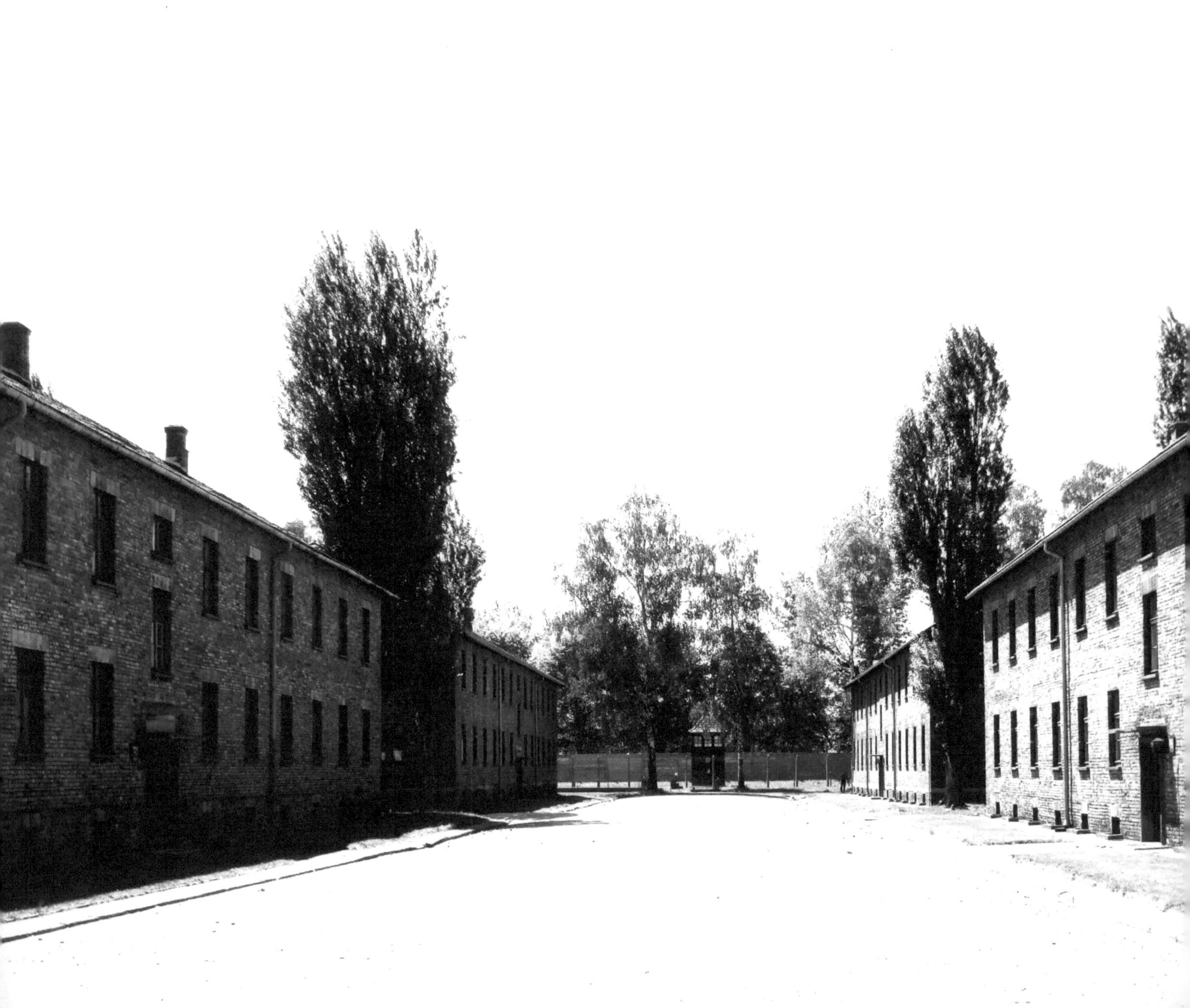

Our curious group did usually,
wonder like we would normally,
filed in and out we did instead.

Many other Crematoriums and Gas chambers were built as the Nazis were unable to keep up with their own efficiency.

Operation Reinhard,[1] in 1942 alone killed 1,274,166 people.

24,733	Majdanek death camp
101,370	Sobibór death camp
434,508	Bełżec death camp
713,555	Treblinka death camp

The total Operation Reinhard killings at the death camps at the completion in 1943 are estimated at 1.7 million[2] Jews. In Auschwitz alone the holocaust claimed 1,100,000 people (200,000 of which were children, 1,000,000 were Jews)[3] of the total estimated 6 million Jews killed, in the "final solution."

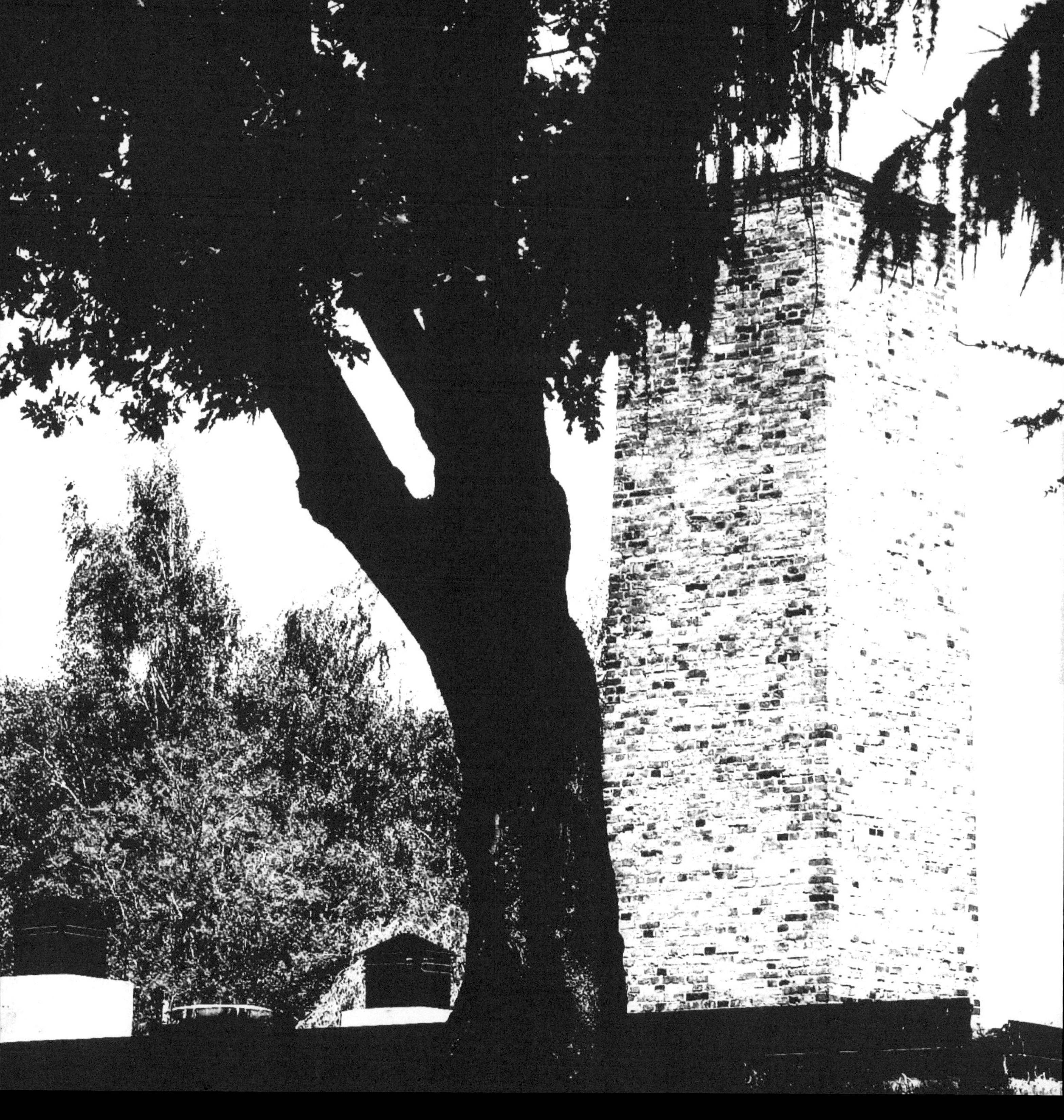

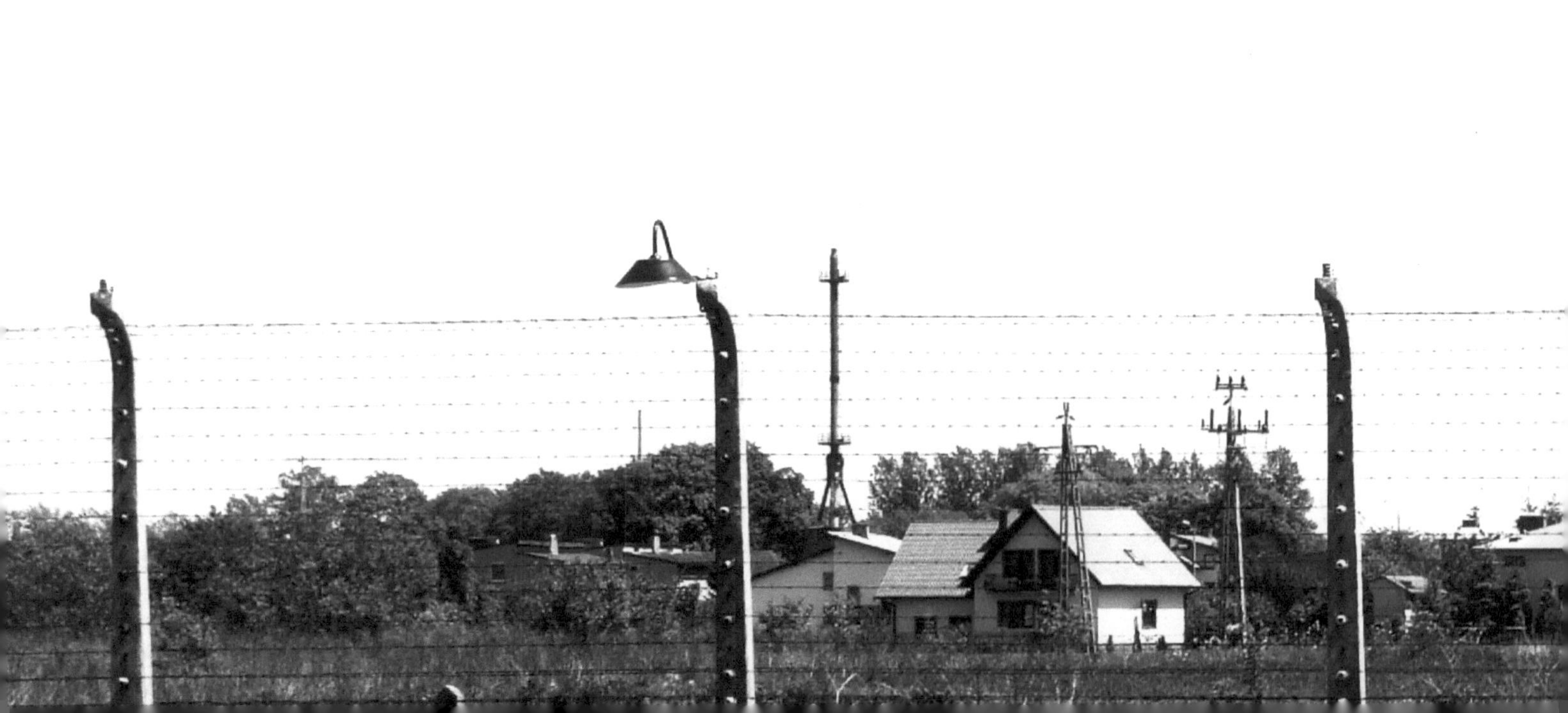

How one survives as guide in hell,
facts mechanically given well,
letting I peer not her soul.

Without inflection lifeless feeling,
proofs recited without thinking,
confronting this not today.

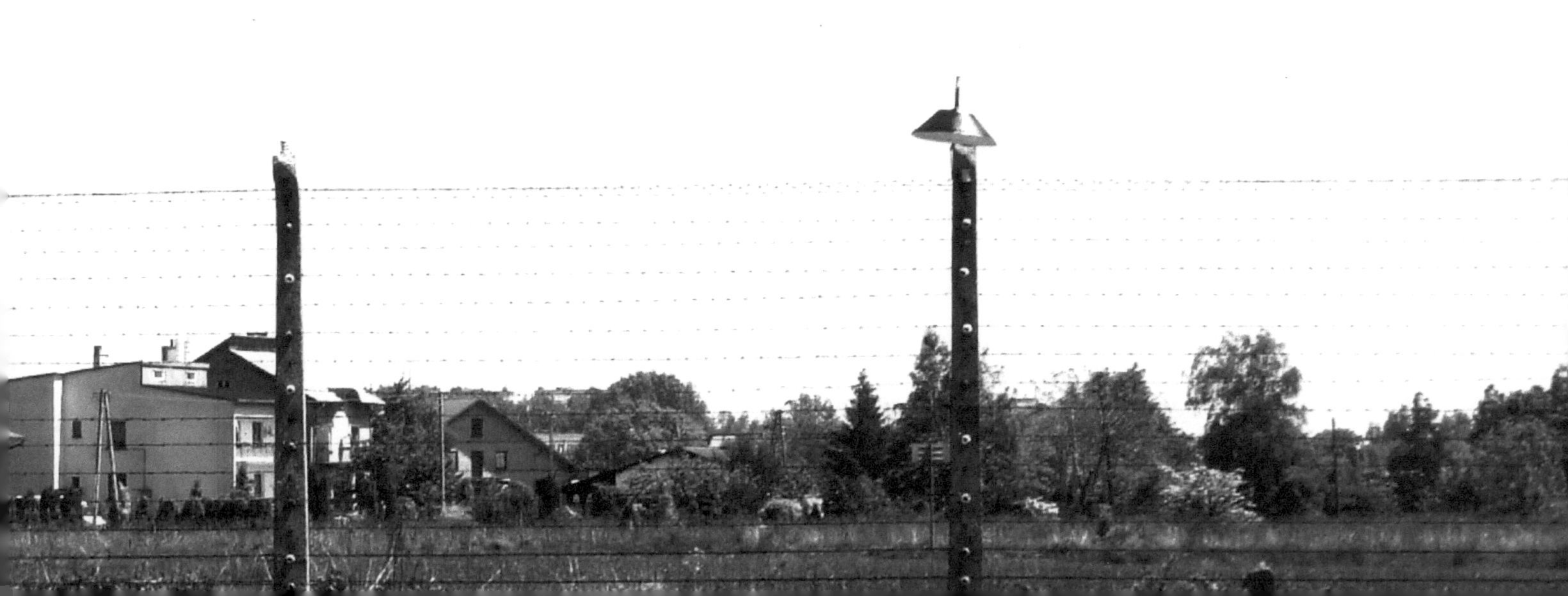

By the end of 1944, the Red army was approaching. The Nazis began removing the traces of the crimes they had committed. They destroyed the documents, dismantled buildings, and demolished all but one of the remaining crematoriums and gas chambers.[1] Orders for the final liquidation of the camp came in mid January 1945.[2] Prisoners capable of marching were sent deep into the Third Reich in late January, at the moment the Soviet soldiers were liberating Kraków 60 km away. 56,000 prisoners were sent out on January 17-21 in what is known as the "death march.[3]" Many died. Those who survived found themselves in another concentration camp. On January 27, the Red army soldiers liberated a few thousand prisoners left behind in the camp.[4]

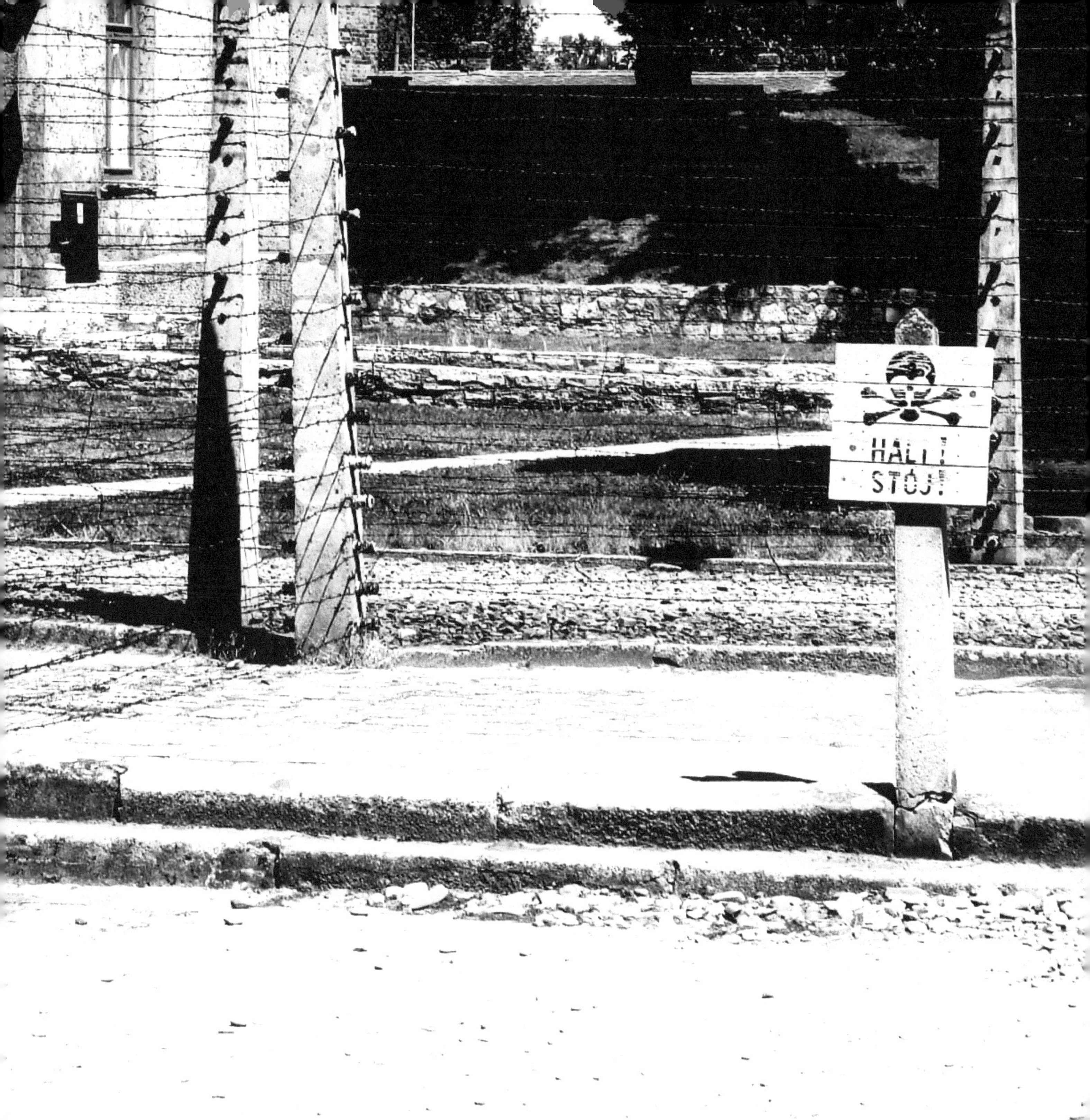
HALT!
STÓJ!

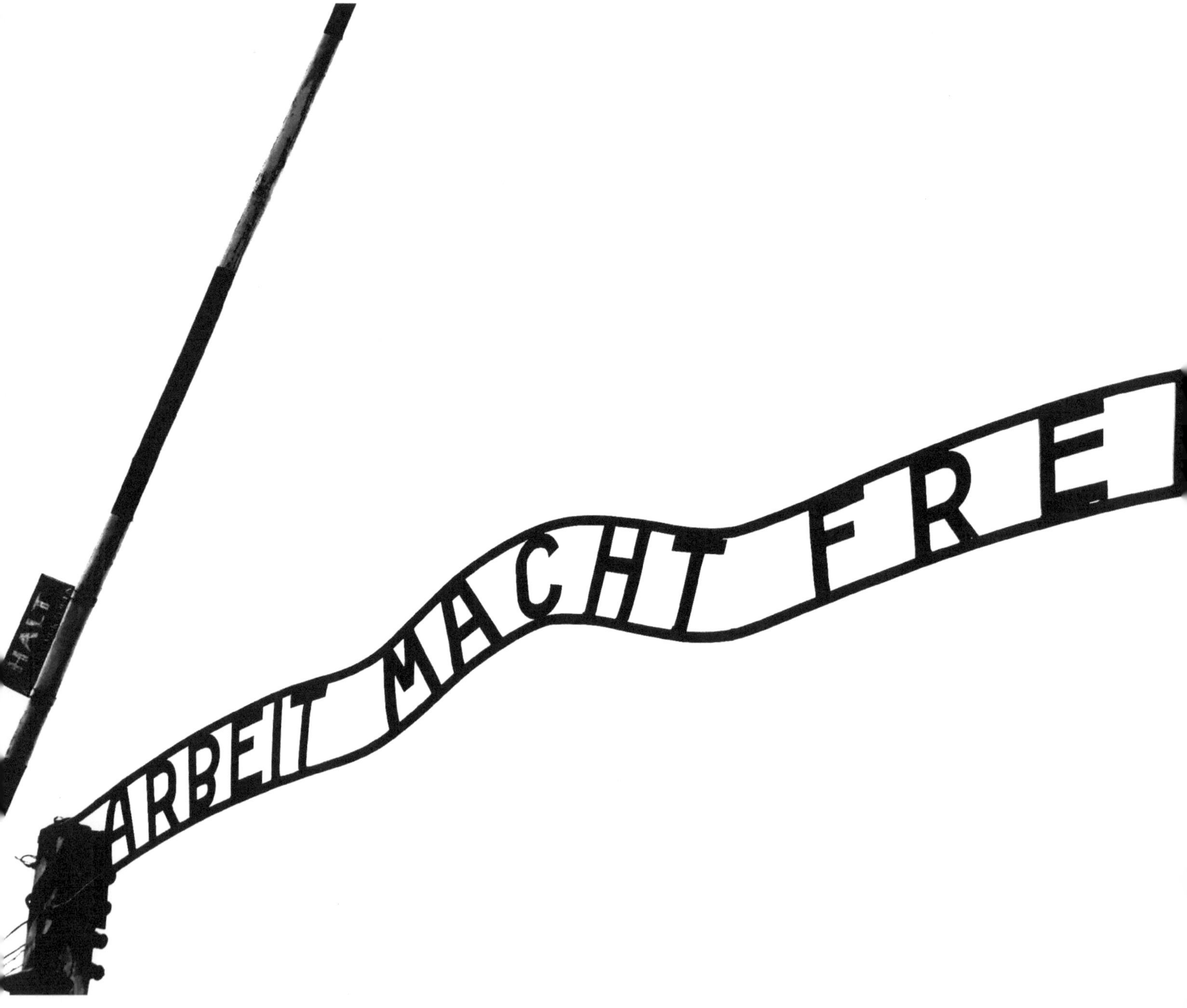

HALT
ARBEIT MACHT FRE

Questions required internalizing,
think not now about what I'm hearing,
such is the horror of my thoughts.

Afterwards

By the time the Nazis capitulated to the allied forces, Hitler committed suicide[1] while the Red Army was approaching the Reichstag, on April 30th 1945. Less than one month later, Himmler[2] followed his former leader's example and committed suicide by poison capsule, leaving Höss hiding his identity and living in a farm stable. Without saying a word, Höss was hung behind the crematorium in Auschwitz I in April 1947 after being sentenced to death in the Nürnberg trials. Much of what is known about the camps today Höss wrote in his memoirs[3] during his imprisonment.

On May 7, 1945 World War II in Europe ends, along with the greatest holocaust mankind has committed. Six million Jews where murdered, as well as another ten million non-combatants killed[4] by the Nazis.

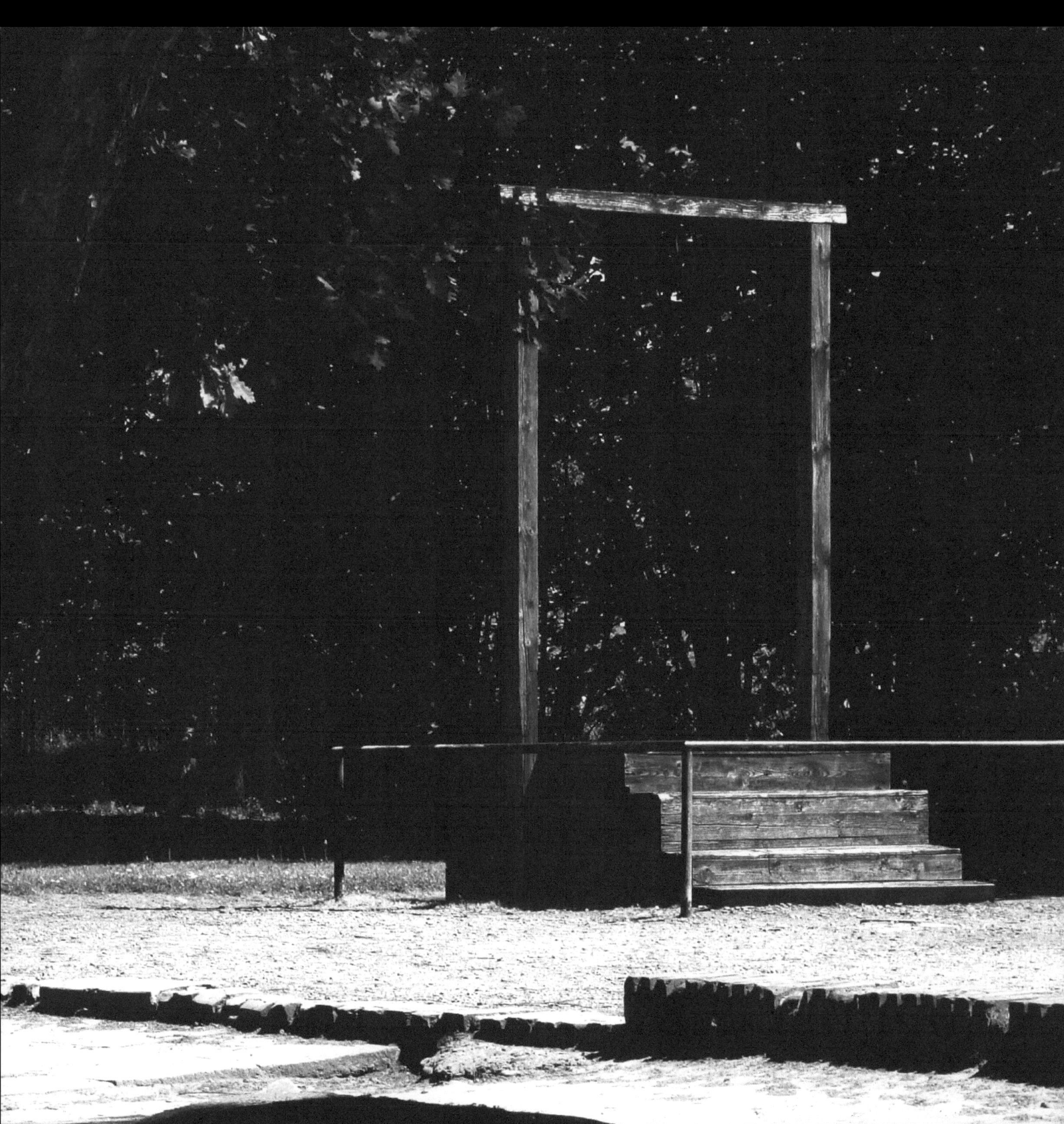

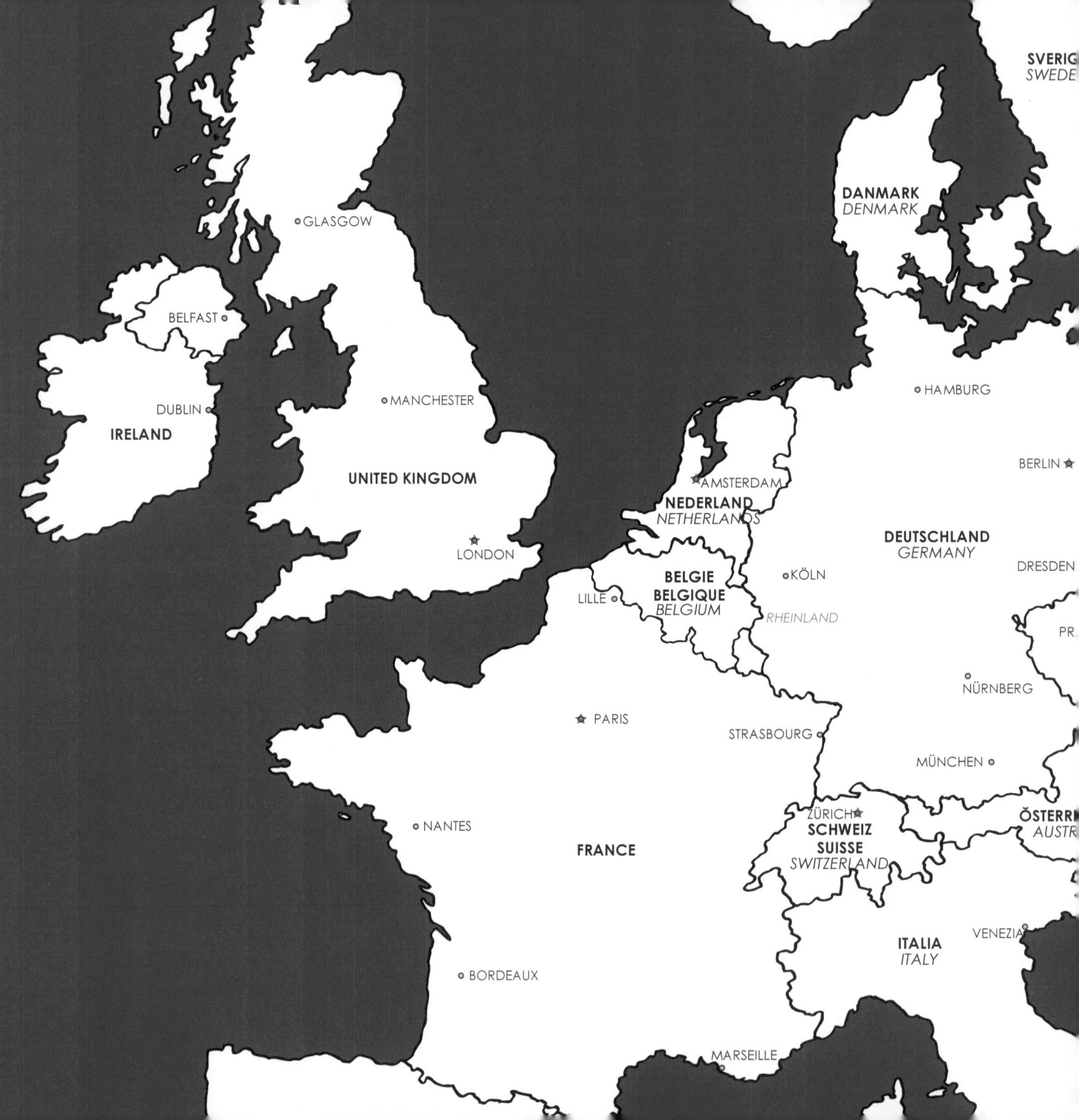

SVERIG
SWEDE
DANMARK
DENMARK
GLASGOW
BELFAST
HAMBURG
MANCHESTER
DUBLIN
IRELAND
BERLIN
AMSTERDAM
UNITED KINGDOM
NEDERLAND
NETHERLANDS
DEUTSCHLAND
GERMANY
LONDON
DRESDEN
BELGIE
BELGIQUE
BELGIUM
KÖLN
LILLE
RHEINLAND
PR
NÜRNBERG
PARIS
STRASBOURG
MÜNCHEN
ZÜRICH
SCHWEIZ
SUISSE
SWITZERLAND
ÖSTERR
AUSTR
NANTES
FRANCE
VENEZIA
ITALIA
ITALY
BORDEAUX
MARSEILLE

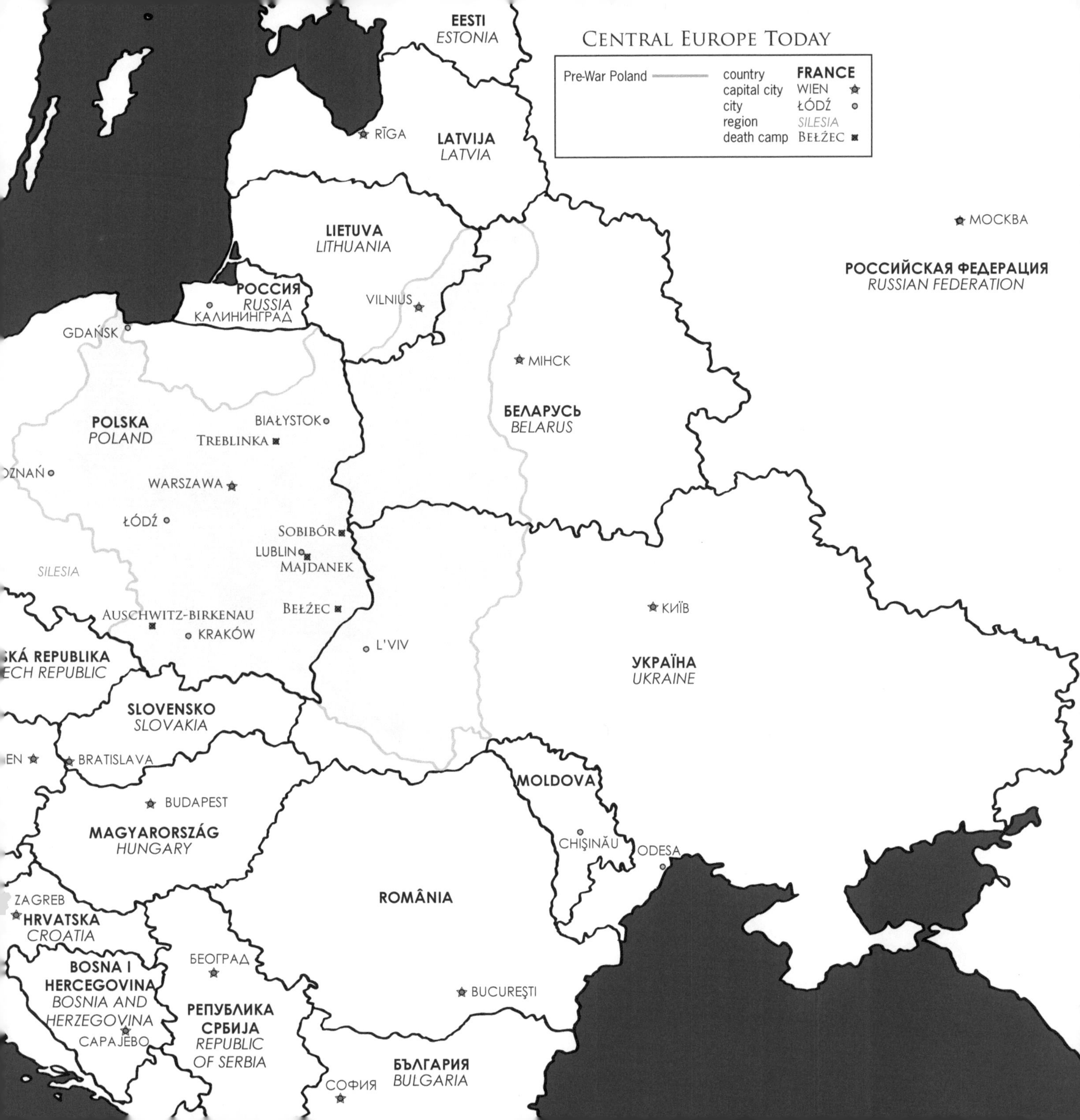
CENTRAL EUROPE TODAY
Pre-War Poland
country FRANCE
capital city WIEN
city ŁÓDŹ
region SILESIA
death camp BEŁŻEC
EESTI
ESTONIA
RĪGA
LATVIJA
LATVIA
LIETUVA
LITHUANIA
РОССИЯ
RUSSIA
КАЛИНИНГРАД
VILNIUS
МОСКВА
РОССИЙСКАЯ ФЕДЕРАЦИЯ
RUSSIAN FEDERATION
GDAŃSK
МІНСК
БЕЛАРУСЬ
BELARUS
POLSKA
POLAND
BIAŁYSTOK
TREBLINKA
ZNAŃ
WARSZAWA
ŁÓDŹ
SOBIBÓR
LUBLIN
MAJDANEK
SILESIA
BEŁŻEC
AUSCHWITZ-BIRKENAU
KRAKÓW
L'VIV
КИЇВ
УКРАЇНА
UKRAINE
SKÁ REPUBLIKA
ECH REPUBLIC
SLOVENSKO
SLOVAKIA
EN
BRATISLAVA
MOLDOVA
BUDAPEST
MAGYARORSZÁG
HUNGARY
CHIŞINĂU
ODESA
ZAGREB
HRVATSKA
CROATIA
ROMÂNIA
BOSNA I
HERCEGOVINA
BOSNIA AND
HERZEGOVINA
БЕОГРАД
BUCUREŞTI
РЕПУБЛИКА
СРБИЈА
REPUBLIC
OF SERBIA
САРАЈЕВО
БЪЛГАРИЯ
BULGARIA
СОФИЯ

NOTES ON THE TEXT

Station 1 (page 8)
1. Gilbert, "The Holocaust," 23.
2. Ibid., 24, quoted from Hitlers August 13, 1920 speech in a München beer cellar.
3. Ibid., 31.
4. Laqueur, "Holocaust Encyclopedia," xxiii.

Station 2 (page 12)
1. Rees, "Auschwitz," 1.
2. Gilbert, "The Holocaust," 121.
3. Gutman, "Anatomy of the Auschwitz death camp," 6. For "offenses [that] were 'relatively light and definitely correctable.'"

Station 3 (page 16)
1. Gutman, "Anatomy of the Auschwitz death camp," 6.
2. Swiebocka, "Auschwitz-Birkenau," 8
3. Gilbert, "The Holocaust," 122.

Station 4 (page 20)
1. Rees, "Auschwitz," 62.
2. Gilbert, "The Holocaust," 286.

Station 5 (page 24)
1. Rees, "Auschwitz," 9.
2. Ibid., 33.

Station 6 (page 28)
1. Laqueur, "Holocaust Encyclopedia," 36.
2. Rees, "Auschwitz," 109-153.

Station 7 (page 32)
1. Laqueur, "Holocaust Encyclopedia," 36.
2. Rees, "Auschwitz," 81.
3. Ibid., 83.

Station 8 (page 36)
1. Laqueur, "Holocaust Encyclopedia," 37.
2. Rees, "Auschwitz," 101.
3. Ibid., 81-82.

Station 9 (page 40)

1. Gutman, "Anatomy of the Auschwitz death camp," 31, 52
2. Ibid., 360-361.

Station 10 (page 44)

1. There is conflicting information as to the block # for the "death block." The Auschwitz Museum designates it as Block 11, in which there is a memorial to St. Kolbe.

Station 11 (page 48)

1. Gutman, "Anatomy of the Auschwitz death camp," 83. Wiernicki "War in the shadow of Auschwitz," 85
2. Gutman, "Anatomy of the Auschwitz death camp," 162
3. Rees, "Auschwitz," 298.

Station 12 (page 54)

1. Gutman, "Anatomy of the Auschwitz death camp," 26-27
2. Ibid., 26.
3. Look at Nomberg-Przytyk, Spiegelman, Wiernicki, and Wiesel.
4. Gutman, "Anatomy of the Auschwitz death camp," 6

Station 13 (page 58)

1. Rees, "Auschwitz," 164.
2. Laqueur, "Holocaust Encyclopedia," 500.
3. Rees, "Auschwitz," xxi and 299.

Station 14 (page 62)

1. Gutman, "Anatomy of the Auschwitz death camp," 174
2. Rees, "Auschwitz," 256
3. Ibid., 262-263.
4. Gutman, "Anatomy of the Auschwitz death camp," 32

Afterward (page 66)

1. Rees, "Auschwitz," 270.
2. Ibid., 271
3. Ibid., 290.
4. Gilbert, "The Holocaust," 824

Selected Bibliography

I list the major works and writings that I consulted; it does not include all of the works and sources. This list does include works on Auschwitz and the Holocaust, not used as sources for the text, but that are interesting in their presentation of the subject.

Bererbaum, Michael. *The World Must Know: the history of the Holocaust as told in the United States Holocaust Memorial Museum. Boston*: Little, Brown & Company, 1993, ISBN 0-316-09135-9

Friedlander, Albert H., comp. *Out of the Whirlwind: A reader of Holocaust literature*. New York: Schocken Books, 1976, ISBN 0-8052-0517-9

Gilbert, Martin. *The Holocaust: A history of the Jews of Europe during the Second World War*. New York: Owl Book, 1985, ISBN 978-0-8050-0348-2

Gutman, Israel. *Anatomy of the Auschwitz death camp. Bloomington* : Published in association with the United States Holocaust Memorial Museum, Washington, D.C. [by] Indiana University Press, 1998, c1994, ISBN 0-253-20884-x

Kaczkowski, Adam. *Bramy Tragedii*. Warszawa: Wydownictwo "Sporti Turystyka", 1989, ISBN 83-217-2683-6

Landau, Ronnie S. *Studying the Holocaust: Issues, Readings and Documents*. New York: Routledge, 1998, ISBN 0-415-16144-4

Laqueur, Walter, and Judith Tydor Baumel, ed. *The Holocaust Encyclopedia*. New Haven: Yale University Press, 2001, ISBN 0-300-08432-3

Levi, Primo, Leonardo De Benedetti, and Robert S.C. Gordan, ed. *Auschwitz Report*. Trans. Judith Woolf. New York: Verso, 2006, ISBN 978-84467-092-5

Nomberg-Przytyk, Sara, 1915. *Auschwitz : true tales from a grotesque land*. Chapel Hill : University of North Carolina Press, c1985, ISBN 0-8078-4160-9

Rees, Laurence. *Auschwitz: A new History*. New York: Public Affairs, 2005, ISBN 978-1-58648-357-9

Singer, Michael A. ed. *Humanity at the Limit: the impact of the Holocaust experience on Jews and Christians*. Bloomington: Indiana University Press, 2000, ISBN 0-253-33739-9

Spiegelman, Art. *MAUS: a survivor's tale I: my father bleeds history*. New York: Pantheon Books, 1986, ISBN 0-394-74723-2

———. *MAUS: a survivor's tale II: and here my troubles began*. New York: Pantheon Books, 1991, ISBN 0-679-72977-1

Świebocka, Teresa, comp., Pinderska-Lech, comp., Jarko Mensfelt, comp. *Auschwitz-Birkenau: History and the Present*. Trans. Adam Czasak. Oswiecim: Auschwitz-Birkenau State Museum, 2007, ISBN: 978-83-60210-41-3

Wiernicki, John. *War in the shadow of Auschwitz: memoirs of a Polish resistance fighter and survivor of the death camps*. Syracuse University Press, 2001, ISBN 0-8156-0722-9

Wiesel, Elie. *Night*. Trans. Marion Wiesel. New York: Hill and Wang, 2006, ISBN 978-0-374-50001-6

Illustrations

ACKNOWLEDGMENTS

Thanks foremost to Professors Rick and Laura Brown of MassArt and Handshouse Studio for repeatedly inviting me to participate in their endeavors; I would not have gone to Poland without them. Thanks to Massachusetts College of Art, the Colleges of the Fenway, and Wentworth Institute of Technology for their financial support in my travels. Thanks to all of the students who traveled with me; our conversations were invaluable. To the tour guides whom day in and day out live through reciting such awful stories and facts. Vanessa Nason, for proofreading the rough draft, and especially to Nurit Zuker for her editing of the end transcript. Thanks also to my colleagues for their time and interest in developing this book, for their attendance and responses to my lecture (which became the groundwork for this book) and for putting up with the random facts that I relate to them on a daily basis. Thanks also to the Auschwitz-Birkenau State Museum for their kind permission to photograph at the museum.

www.ingramcontent.com/pod-product-compliance
Lightning Source LLC
LaVergne TN
LVHW070138110826
845147LV00002B/279